After All These Years

After All These Years

Our Gypsy journey continues

Maggie Smith-Bendell

University of Hertfordshire Press

First published in Great Britain in 2013 by
University of Hertfordshire Press
College Lane
Hatfield
Hertfordshire AL10 9AB

British Library Cataloguing in Publication Data
A catalogue record for this book is available from the British Library

ISBN 978-1-907396-96-0

Design by Mathew Lyons
Printed in Great Britain by Hobbs the Printers Ltd, Totton, Hampshire

.

I dedicate this book to my husband Terry, who never once tried to take the Gypsy out of me, but instead embraced my lifestyle, while keeping his own intact. He gave me a gold band on my finger and two wonderful sons – Michael and Jason. He encouraged me in every way to do the work on behalf of my people that I chose to do, to make them a better life, gain health care and education and somewhere to live. He gave me a love I had never known and the will to carry on after I lost him in death.

Thank you, my plum, for your deep love and support. And most of all for being my Gorgie Mush for fifty years.

Contents

1. Summer Months 1
2. Childhood Days 13
3. A Christmas Remembered 18
4. Near Death Experience 31
5. Our Beginnings 38
6. A Change of Lifestyle 47
7. Looking Back 60
8. Life on the Road 65
9. Bridgwater Fair 82
10. Pride of the Road 96
11. The Arrival of Winter 104
12. Heading into a New Year 115
13. Mixed Marriage 123
14. Our Life Together 143
15. My Romani Rye's Funeral 164
16. Memories of Happier Times 174
17. In the Hop Gardens Once Again 183
18. Springtime Comes Around Again 197

Acknowledgements 203
Glossary of Romani Words 205
Reading List: Romani History 207

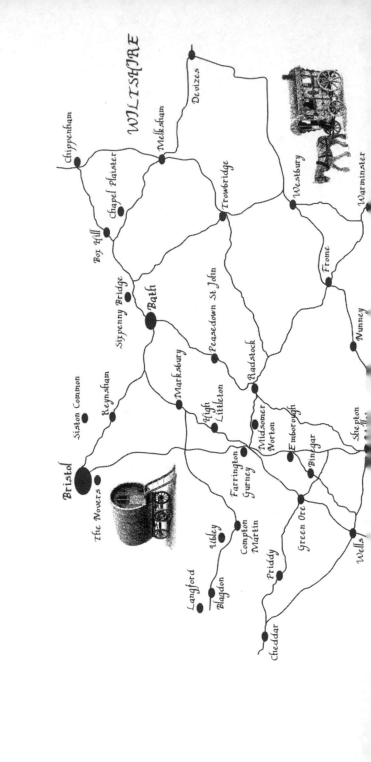

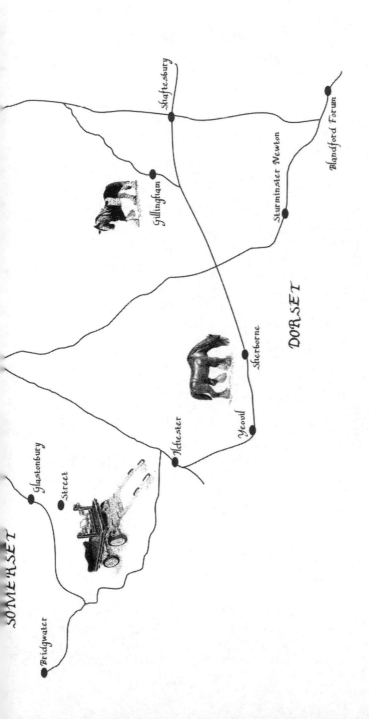

SOMERSET

DORSET

Bridgwater

Glastonbury

Street

Ilchester

Yeovil

Sherborne

Gillingham

Shaftesbury

Sturminster Newton

Blandford Forum

Chapter One

Summer Months

I WAS LUCKY ENOUGH to be born into a unique race of people, the Romani Gypsy race. Deep in the heart of Somerset, my family lived a nomadic lifestyle, as did our ancestors for hundreds of generations before us. Steeped in the culture and customs of our forefathers, we lived by tradition, travelling the roads and lanes not only of Somerset but of Devon, Dorset, Wiltshire and Herefordshire. Often we strayed into other counties too, either by intention or on a whim, seeking the all-important work that kept body and soul together. Mostly this was field work, or we'd hawk our wares and swag round the settled community's doors: handmade wooden flowers and clothes pegs, scrubbing brushes, bootlaces and wax-paper roses, medicines and potions. We picked the edible wild berries to sell in season too, as well as mushrooms and many other things. The grand horses that was bred from our own faithful working stock was brought on and broke in as drivers and sold at our Gypsy horse fairs.

Thus we travelled and grew up. We had a peaceful sort of life. We entertained ourselves with singing and dancing. Children had very few toys if any – there was no room to carry such things. But then, come to think on it, we had no real need of them: we had all the trees, farmers' gates to swing on and horses, dogs and little bantam chicks to play with.

Once we had pulled off the road and done our chores (such as fetching wood and water), our time was our own. Summer evenings would see us out round the fields and lanes picking baskets full of wild flowers for our mams to sell, or collecting the new shoots of herbs to make medicine. We never had a dull moment, really. Life was full to the brim. It was our life, the only one we knew, and the only one we could wish for. It may sound as though we chavvies (children) had very little time for ourselves – but that was far from being the case.

Our special time was when we gathered and sat round the yog (fire) – or when me Dad would whisper, 'Keep quiet and follow me, I got some thing to show yis.' It could be anything from a nest of young birds to a badger set where the very young badgers were at play or even a nest of hedgehogs filled with tiny young ones. And he would tell us all about the animals that he had shown us.

This was the way we learned, as he passed his knowledge of wildlife on to us. Life was *very* interesting: each day brought new things to see and learn about. As for working alongside our parents in the fields and hop gardens, we never really thought about it in terms of *having* to do it – we expected and accepted that it was part of how we lived. For instance, when we pulled onto the pea fields the first thing we chavvies looked for was buckets to pick the peas in, because buckets filled quicker than the pea nets and we felt we picked more that way.

As for having time to play, we had loads of free time, mostly in the evenings when we could wander off and do our own thing, so long as we didn't get in any trouble such as falling in a pond or ditch – because if there was any water about we were sure to find it. It drew us like magnets.

I've always said we had the best of childhoods.

Looking back, there were three main stages to my life. The first was being reared and raised within a close, loving family, taught from a very early age how to get me living and how to survive by working the land and using our own Gypsy skills. I experienced the joy of watching me Dad and all the other men whittle beautiful flowers from an elder stick. Of sitting round our yog and seeing dozens upon dozens of wooden clothes pegs falling to the ground, finished and ready to sell. Of the smell of herbs simmering in an old black pot kept for just this very purpose to make the potions and medicines – some for us to keep for our own use and some to sell or barter away.

Living in the open air meant our cooking smells floated far and wide, giving many a gorgie (non-Romani) hunger pangs as they passed by. My memory of my childhood is fresh in me mind's eye – the feeling of being looked after and safe from harm, feeling peckish but never what you would call hungry. Oh no, there was no hunger – the skills of the men and boys enabled them to catch fresh meat each day and then the best of cooks, our mothers, saw to all our needs. The Romani women were always ready to go out calling to earn bread money and could stretch a shilling a mile – filling her chavvies' bellies would be uppermost in her mind, and after that maybe she'd get a bit of baccy for her man.

Spring and summer were the favourite times. Spring would kind of wake us up and bring the idea of setting off travelling to the front of our minds. Spring would mean new paint on the wagons. Mares would be waiting the last few weeks to have their foals. The long, dark winter nights and cold days would finally be shook off. It was a new beginning, waiting for the wild flowers to spring into life: snowdrops, daffies, bluebells, primroses and cowslips – all would be gathered in turn, bunched up and hawked round doors. And the little wild strawberries would be picked and used to colour and flavour medicines, as would the wild, sweet-smelling violets, especially the white ones. All through the year something or other would come into season to be picked and used for the good of all of us.

Sometimes we'd sell nosegays of buttercups and dandelions tied up with herbs – these two plants which everyone seems to think of as weeds but which should be given at least a second glance at close quarters. They really are beautiful flowers and so bright in their colours. The dandelion can be used in all sorts of ways which I am not at liberty to disclose. The reason I'm not at liberty to disclose these ways is that the herbs and plants we blend with them to make medicines and potions are known to us Romanies by different names from those of the settled community. If folks tried to copy a recipe they could very well pick the wrong plants and make themselves really ill instead of better. I can tell you that the old dandelion was used to make drinks, and the flower stem, which contains a sticky milky substance, was used with a mixture of other plants to make potions for horse ailments.

But I don't think my community would be very happy if I wrote down any of these recipes. They have been closely guarded for hundreds of generations. It's their private knowledge and it's not for me to tell their secrets, so this knowledge will stay in the past, as it should. But we made full use of it when travelling the roads. Knowledge is a wonderful thing and Gypsies had a great deal of knowledge, especially about plants and their healing powers. This knowledge was not shared with the house-dwelling community; it was secret to the Romanies and a great deal of it is still closely guarded today. There is still so much people could learn from us, if we shared our secret knowledge.

The joy of being alive when I woke at dawn on a spring morning, with the songs of the birds and the smoke from our yog. Those spring dawns were a picture. Everything was green and fresh to the yock (eye). Beautiful wild flowers covered in early morning dew filled the hedgerows, banks and fields.

The best part of the day was lighting a big yog between seven and eight o'clock, cooking a fried breakfast and warming up round the flames: thick bacon sizzles in the cast-iron pan that hangs from the old kettle-iron. Sweet-smelling wood burns brightly on the yog. The kettle sings in the embers, ready to be poured on the tea leaves in the huge enamel teapot. That teapot's big enough to fill many cups, once the tea has been left to soak, as we say.

These are the sights that greeted us each and every day as we climbed out the wagon and ambled to the yog for breakfast.

Bellies full to the brim, me and me Mam would set off to hawk the doors of the local house-dwellers, offering our bunches of fresh wild flowers for sale or a few gross of clothes pegs. Meanwhile me Dad stayed close by our wagon and grys (horses), looking after the rest of the family and making the next day's pegs or wooden flowers. Every one of us pulled our weight – and pulled together.

The summer months were grand too. We chavvies could stay up later at night and wake up to the perfume of wild honeysuckle and the dog rose, for the wild perfume was best at night and in the early morning. Wildlife is dear to us still: each tree and bush had its own uses for us – to make medicines or on the yog to keep us warm – and of course the wild meat that fed us.

Autumn was the time of year when old Mother Nature thought, 'These Gypsies have had it too kushti [good]. I'll give them a taste of what's to come, give them a bit of cold, wet and frosty weather to train them up for winter. I'll blow the leaves off the trees to take their shelter and harden them up for all the snow I aim to throw their way.' Oh yes, Mother Nature played a big part in our daily lives. Winter could be a wonderland: if luck was with us, deep snow would see us tucked away near a farm where the men of our family group would work for the farmer mush (man).

While the older family members grumbled about the snow and its drawbacks, I loved it. I enjoyed its beauty, its crispy glittering whiteness.

During the day it would shine in the sunlight, but at night when there was only the glow of the candlelight in the wagon and the yog outside, the snow was a grand sight to see. It would gleam and light up the land as far as the yock could see.

My childhood had its bad times, such as when me Mam forced me and my older brother Alfie to go to school. How we hated being parted from the family wagon and grys, locked away for no good reason within four walls. And to top it all, the teachers never wanted us in their old noisy schools, so it was a waste of good time.

And we had sad times. Death has a habit of visiting my race too soon. Babies died at birth; mothers died birthing; children died by drowning or for the lack of medical help. And the old yog brought many deaths to young chavvies who caught themselves alight getting a warm from the fire. Me Dad lost a young sister to the yog. The death rate was high among Traveller children. Some would fall under the wheels of their wagons as they travelled – because we chavvies saw no danger and trouble often followed our antics. Accidents happened – silly, tragic accidents, but happen they did, and took the lives of the young. Parents spent a deal of time warning their offspring, 'Don't do this, don't do that, mind the road, don't go near the river, don't climb the trees.' Of so very many warnings that we had rammed into our heads we generally took little heed until it was too late.

But all in all we really did have the best of childhoods. Did we not have good, caring parents and the whole countryside to play in? And all the good life we chavvies had, it was our families that made it so.

The second stage of me life was when, at twenty years of age, I met and married a gorgie mush. Fresh out the army he was and full of life. He had deep feelings for me – he was to tell me it was love at first sight. All me life I had known a love of and for me family, but nothing anywhere near what was happening to me now. This was new to me, this was the love of just one person for another, not the shared family love I was used to.

By falling for me mush I hurt me parents to the quick. I had gone against my traditions and culture and married my gorgie mush as quick as lightning. He showed me a different kind of love and a different way of life from that of my heritage, and he helped me to have the best of both worlds.

The third stage of me life, and one that has lasted many years, was when I became a Gypsy activist, working for Gypsy families and trying to gain planning permission for private Gypsy sites. I seemed to be very successful at it and I really enjoyed the work – it also meant that I got to meet the younger generations of families I had travelled with when I was young, renewing old friendships. This gave me Mam a great deal of pleasure while she still lived – and as a result we got in touch with relatives we never knew we had. Such as Denny and Sallyann Smith of Cheltenham – close relatives of me Dad and a wonderful old-fashioned family who still built their own horse-drawn wagons. Alas, me Dad had passed away long afore so he never learned of their existence. Had he done, I know he and them would have been drunk as handcarts for a week.

It wasn't easy breaking in to the world of planning. It drove me mad at times because I got so frustrated – my lack of knowledge knew no bounds, but I was determined to learn. I was desperate to help my community in any way I could and the best way to start was by helping to provide homes, permanent bases.

I had a good friend and teacher, Mr Brian Cox of South West Law in Bristol, who was a well-known Gypsy planning solicitor. He took me under his wing and taught me right from wrong. And my dear husband Terry gave me all the encouragement he could – and picked me up when it got me down. He would say, 'If you believe in what you're

Me with solicitor Brian Cox on a site visit during a planning appeal.

doing, my old gal, learn to roll with the knockbacks. Shake yourself off and get back in the fight.'

This, then, is my story – told in the hope that by reading it people will see us Gypsies in a new light and come to a better understanding of my race, stop viewing us with suspicion and offer us their trust for the first time since we came to these shores hundreds of years ago. I would like people to see us as a race apart, a self-supporting community, who live by tradition and culture as far as today's society allows. And I also want both them and my own people to know the price we have paid for being born and bred in the Romani community.

This is my second book on my life and community. *Our Forgotten Years* was published in 2009 by University of Hertfordshire Press (and later reprinted by Abacus as *Rabbit Stew and a Penny or Two).* I feel I need to keep writing because there is still so much of my life and culture I need to share, not only with the settled community but with my own as well. Our way of life has changed so much since my travelling days on the roads. I need to tell the younger generations of my own community how it was just sixty years ago and how things have changed for us in that short time. Young Romani Gypsies of today only hear our travelling tales from their grandparents and can't get their heads round the idea of living in wagons and being on the move on a daily basis: spending most of that life sitting round outside fires; eating all our meals in the open air come rain, sun, snow or winds; hanging washing out to dry on a hedge after our mams had sat for hours scrubbing the clothes in a tin bath and boiling the whites in a bucket hung over the yog; making our living by using the real old skills such as making chrysanthemum flowers from elder, using brightly coloured crepe paper to make lifelike wax roses or cutting clothes pegs from the hazel bush; working from dawn till tea time out on the land, in all winds and weathers.

It's hard for them to visualise this way of life as they sit in their smart caravans and mobile homes of today (either living on a local authority or private site), watching a flat screen TV and with the latest mobile phone stuck to their ears. They know nothing of the free feeling of pulling on to the open common land in a brightly painted wagon pulled by a beautiful sturdy coloured gry; collecting wood fallen from the old tall trees and dragging it back to light the yog so a very tasty meal can be cooked and eaten out in God's clean air; enjoying the love of that closeknit and extended family and being told the tales of bygone days.

We must not forget these grand old days and the precious memories of a lifestyle that's only now a memory in our old minds and an old tale to tell today's young ones.

First and foremost, my race are a very private community of people: we like to keep our private business and our culture safe within our own community. This is an important part of our make-up, part and parcel of our unique way of life. It's not that we Romanies are unsociable – far from it: we need to integrate to earn our living. We are family-orientated and do our utmost to keep it that way. In all creeds and races family ties are precious, but in our community they are even more so. We cling together because really bad, unforgettable things happened to us in past generations – things told again and again in our old tales. This has bonded us together for ever so that now we are one of the toughest groups alive.

There's a chapter about these terrible things later in this book to help people understand what has made us this way.

For generations people have been fascinated by my race, the Romani Gypsies. Once a strange mush stopped to chat to us while we were all sat round the fire one night. He was full of questions, too many questions to suit Grandad.

'What is you after?' asked Grandad. 'Why is you asking all these questions?'

'Because I wants to write a book about you people.' This is how Grandad told it.

'Write a book about we lot?'

'Yes,' said the mush.

'Well take my advice and go away and write about somebody else.'

'But your life and ways needs to be wrote down,' said the mush.

'Mister, the only thing going down is you if you don't scram. Now git going or I'll help you on your way...'

This little episode gave us a new subject to discuss: 'What the hell do the mush want to write about we lot for? We don't interfere with they old gorgies.'

'No,' said me Dad, 'but they sure likes to interfere with us.'

Looking back now, that mush could have been one of the well-known writers of books about the Gypsy race – such as George Borrow or John Sampson, whose books I myself now collect – and I often think how hard it must have been for such people to get their information out of my lot, because we kept our private lives very private indeed. Nosy people were not made welcome by families such as ours. As far as we know, me Grandad did not end up in any books – only mine – which is a great pity for he had a character as big as himself and his knowledge alone would have filled many pages and benefited others. But we respect the wish to keep a lot of the old knowledge within our community – after all, it's our little bit of heritage.

One or two individuals did manage to get to know some of the old families and travelled alongside them as the Gypsies went about their daily life. These people then wrote books about their experiences of life on the road – or at least about as much of our traditions and lifestyle as we allowed them to learn. It's all very well for people to write books about us, but have they got to know the *real* Gypsies? Have they taken the time to learn of our early history, starting from when we first came to Scotland and England way back in the fourteenth century? Do they know about the persecution our people suffered?

Grandad Jim with his second wife Annie.

I myself am descended from some of the oldest Romani Gypsy families in this country. On me Dad's side it was the Smiths and Butlers: me Granny Emma was a Smith and dear old Grandad was a Butler – Dannal Butler, well-known in the Wiltshire and Somerset areas. Me Mam on the other hand was a Black on her mam's side – Minnie Black – and me Grandad was old Jim Small from Devonshire. These families have been resident in England for centuries. When I tell you about those Gypsies of long ago, it is my ancestors and those of every Romani Gypsy in this country that I speak of.

Chapter Two

Childhood Days

FIRST OF ALL LET ME TELL YOU something of my life, travelling the highways with my family, the Smiths. My experiences was typical of most all Gypsies travelling the countryside in the 1940s and 1950s.

I was born down in the West Country in 1941 – while my parents were working on the land picking peas for the farmers near Bridgwater in Somerset. Somerset was a beautiful county in which to travel – green and lush in late spring and summer with field after field laid to growing peas, beans, swedes, cabbages, corn, wheat and barley – all manner of food providing work for one and all. Late autumn and winter could be bitter with frosts, high winds, ice and snow which drove us to seek shelter and work on local farms. All year round it was work and more work.

You'd find us picking the dew-soaked peas afore the sun come up – and when it did show its hot old face, we'd be sweating as we bent to pull the allum from the ground, ripping off its green fruits to fill our nets to twenty pound in weight ('allum' is the Romani name for the pea-plant). Then the farmer would weigh them off on his big old iron scales and add them up in a book. Each Friday we would be paid out for the week's labour.

Come autumn, you would most likely find us in the hop gardens of Ledbury – early mornings of cold, wet fog – the high-growing hop vines would drench us as we pulled them down around our heads and shoulders. They could rip your skin off if care wasn't taken.

At times we stopped and pulled in off the road onto the wetlands which lie between Bridgwater and Glastonbury. We'd be surrounded by ditches.

And while we lit the yog and settled down to a welcome rest, we would watch the peat-cutters hard at work, cutting deep spadefuls of dripping wet, black peat and stacking it up to dry. The men would call to each other as they did their backbreaking work, then sit down for a bite to eat and, by the smell of it, a drink of cider made by the local farmers. Me Dad, believe it or not, never got the taste for cider. He was a brown ale drinker, which he drank every chance he got – before we shifted on.

Me Dad, Lenard Smith, was a strong-willed mush. As was me Mam Defiance – known as Little Fiance by other Travellers but called 'My Vie' by me Dad. He gave her the name of Violet after the sweet-smelling little wild flower. That's what you call love.

I love to remember and relive those precious early years of my childhood, when all my family were young and walked with a spring in their step. We'd walk miles each day at the head of our gry while it gently pulled our wagon round the country roads and lanes, singing together for all the world to hear and know we were happy. Yes, we were happy with our lot, the little we had.

As my memories run through me mind so fast, I remember the good, the bad and the ugly times. Dates mean very little; all that matters is that we lived through those times and remember them, because I know in me heart those days will not return. Yes, the odd Romani will take to the road in a wagon, but the law will make sure they keep on the move. It won't ever be like it was, it can't ever be. Those days are gone, those carefree days when we could travel to well-known stopping places and be familiar with every village en route (even if we didn't know their names). But they're etched in me mind.

Each New Year our parents would try to map out the working year. The family would have a chat round the yog and decide well ahead of time where we would go or what was to be done. Disagreements would be argued over and ironed out. But it always seemed to go wrong for one reason or another: a death in the family or the loss of a horse could disrupt the best laid plans and we would need to work around such an event. Just about anything could go wrong at times, but our life compared to that of earlier generations was sweet: we could travel at will, up or down the country, wherever we felt like going.

Life went on in the same old way, seeking and getting field work of every description, bumping in to other Travelling families at the turn of a corner. 'Travelling' and 'Travellers', I write, because that's what we called ourselves – alas, that name has now been taken over by a new breed of people, the New Age Travellers. And we also have more of the Irish Travellers travelling our English counties now, so to keep our identity today we use the word 'Gypsy' but, as you can see, I still call my lot Travellers.

Me Dad used to enjoy getting skimmish by visiting the closest kitcherma (pub) and downing pints of brown ale. That's if they would serve him: 'No Gypsies served here' was a sign that hung in many pub windows. Those signs would make his neck turn red and he'd rant, 'I ain't no Gypsy, I'm a Travelling man – and proud of it.' 'Gypsy' was not a name my community liked to be labelled with. It was the name the gorgie people called us: among ourselves we were Travellers. Back in those days 'Gypsy' still had a ring of shame to it and it was a name used to beat us with. 'You dirty thieving Gyppos,' they called us at every opportunity, which cut us like a knife to the bone, but we hid our feelings and looked back at such people with a look of disgust and pity. That was something we had learned to do to hurt them back – showing them our scorn. We had had it drummed in to us not to be brazen or cheeky to our elders and that meant gorgie elders as well. But at times while out calling with me Mam she would bite back at them.

Knocking at a house to try to sell a few pegs one day in the Fifties, the door was opened by a smallish child. As the door swung open, a nasty dirty smell come zooming out and we could see from the doorway the house was like a pig sty. We stepped back to get a breath of cleaner air as we heard the child call its mother, 'Mummy, it's the Gypsies, it's the Gypsies. Mummy, come quick!'

Then we heard, 'What do the dirty Gyppos want? I won't buy anything off the dirty Gyppos.'

Out the corner of me yock I saw me Mam put her foot in the doorway. Out comes this woman who looked like she ain't washed or combed her hair in a twelvemonth and her child was in the same state. And there was an infant crawling on the floor in a dirty nappy which was the same colour as the old lino that had not been washed in many a year.

'I don't buy off the Gyppos,' the woman shouted at me Mam. 'Now get away from my house, go, go on, get out!'

'I'll tell you something, Missus, I shan't sell you me pegs either. They's far too clean to be in your filthy dirty house. You fair stinks, Missus, and so do your house and children. And you got the cheek to call me and mine names.'

The woman was spitting mad because me Mam had hit the nail on the head. 'Get away,' she screamed, 'or I'll report you to the policeman.'

'You can report me to who you like, but I'll tell you this. They wouldn't even have you in the workhouse because you, Missus, is too dirty.'

As we walked away I grinned up at me Mam. 'You was brazen to that woman back there, Mam.'

Going up the next-door path, the woman already had her door open.

'Here we go again,' I thought, but no such thing.

'Oh my dear,' she said to me Mam, 'I heard you next door and you told her everything I would like to say to her. But her man is a bully and would make my life hell.'

'Well, he never bullied me,' answered me Mam.

'No, my dear, he's off waiting for the pub to open, but she'll tell him when he gets back – and he'll report you to the local bobby. Or come to your camp.'

'Well if he comes to our camp, I shall end up feeling sorry for him. My man will skin him alive.'

The woman was whispering by now. 'I hope your man gives him a good hiding,' she says.

'He will, Ma'am,' answered me Mam.

'It's the flies that upset us in this row,' says the woman.

'Flies?' asks me Mam, who hates flies because they land on hoss turds or dog mess and breed diseases.

'Yes, in the summer she gets millions of flies in her house and they come in ours.'

'Well, next year, when they starts to come in, get a bucket of strong Jeyes Fluid and knock on her door. When she opens it, chuck the lot right through. That'll get rid of her flies. Good day to you, Ma'am,' says me Mam as we walk away, forgetting to sell the woman the pegs.

So you can see why it gets us angry to be called dirty, when most of those that call us names should be put out in their own dustbins for the rubbish tip.

Chapter Three

A Christmas Remembered

I REMEMBER WAKING UP one Christmas morning, full of anticipation and expecting to find great things in the socks that me and me brother Alfie had left hanging on the kettle-iron the night afore. Little Jess (the baby) was still sound a-sutty up in me Mam's bed. Me and our Alfie had built ourselves up to expect many kushti things rammed down inside those little socks, because me Mam had told us over the past few days about this old Christmas mush who would call at the wagon and leave us presents if we were good. He would come in the middle of the night and leave us a surprise.

We climbed out the wagon, pushing and shoving each other till we fell on the thick snowy ground, yocks bigger than our heads as we looked for whatever this Christmas mush had left us.

'Where's our things to then, Dad?' our Alfie wanted to know. 'Where's they presents to, then?'

Me Dad was sat round a fine-burning yog while me Mam was stooping to poke at the frying pan. Me yocks scanned all round the yog – no socks on the kettle-iron now, it was holding the boiling kettle over the flames.

'Come to me, yis two,' called me Mam. 'Come and get your presents old Father Christmas left for yis.' She was holding out the socks towards us. Alfie had a white sugar mouse and a few hazelnuts which I knew we had picked back in the autumn. I ended up with the same.

'But Mam, you said we would get presents and I wanted a ball and dolly fer meself.'

'Yis two gets plenty of balls and toys off the ash bins. Only the other day yis collared a heap of toys off the ash heap – when we pulled in near that one...'

'But they was secondhand and broke,' our Alfie cried.

'But yis still played with 'em,' she said.

I couldn't let it go at that. So I told me Mam, 'Yis two told us some old mush called Christmas was bringing us lots of presents.'

'Well, he must have got lost in the snow,' she said, but I caught the wink she gave me dad.

'Right, come on, our Maggie, we'll take a ganders and dick [look] fer the mush,' shouted our Alfie.

'If yis two don't come and eat this breakfast, I'll give the pair of yis a hiding. Now come on and sit by the warm yog.'

'Come on, my chavvies,' said me Dad, sweet-talking us, 'come over yer by yer old dad.'

Christmas meant very little to us while travelling. The only thing that really sticks in my mind is that we had a special dinner that had a smell of its own: Christmas puddings (spicy apple suet dumplings boiled in the pot) preceded by a goose: they always tried to get a goose, not only for the dinner but to save the grease in a jar to use to rub our chests with, if and when we caught a cough.

So that particular Christmas come and went, while we were snowed up in the lane known by all us Travellers as Old Dannal's Basin in Somerset. For once me Dad had been caught out on the weather (which was a rare happening) and we'd got ourselves trapped in this narrow lane, but within sliding distance of Midsomer Norton and Paulton.

When the farmer come rumbling up the lane on his tractor to feed his cows, he stopped and asked us if all was well.

'I'm in need of a bale or two of hay, and I got money to pay me way,' answered me Dad.

'I'll drop you off one now and one later,' said the farmer mush.

At least our two grys would have a feed for it was bitter cold as the snow had frozen over and crunched when we walked on it.

On his next visit the farmer dropped off the hay and a bag with a loaf of home-baked bread, a lump of cheese and eggs.

'The missus sent this for the kiddies,' he said, 'and three fields along the lane is swedes – help yourselves.'

'Thank you very much, farmer,' said me Dad, having already visited the field for the past few days – the very same swedes was cooking in the pot as he spoke, topped off with a rabbit. But it was kushti to gain permission (the farmer mush would get paid in full for the bit of vegetables we borrowed by having our men work like donkeys on his land: all things in life has to be paid for one way or another).

It would be days afore we could get out the lane and we spent many hours round the yog.

'Mam,' I asked one day, 'who *is* this Christmas mush?'

'When I puts yis in the school you'll soon learn about him.'

'School? We ain't gonna go in no school,' said Alfie.

'Oh yes you is – and learn to write your name.'

'What do I want to write me name for? I knows who I is,' he answered.

Every so often the school would be mentioned again. She would want to put us in one of they old school houses. Years later, when I was twelve or thirteen and could write me name, she told the other Travellers her chavvies was good scholars; it gave her a reason to brag about us.

But just the word 'school' sent shivers up my and our Alfie's backs.

We had a fear on us whenever that word come up. We vowed never to go. What did we need school for?

Once we were able to leave the lane, we headed back up to Wiltshire. On the way we called up the Prince Lane, on the outskirts of the village of Peasedown St John on the old Bath road – where we found Grandad getting ready to leave the lane to travel.

'It's a great pity we both can't travel together,' Grandad said to me Dad.

'I know how it is between me Mum and my Vie,' he replied. 'It's best we take our own road – then there won't be any arguments.'

It was true that me Mam and the old Granny, Emma, rowed like cat and dog. I think me Granny hated me Mam, judging by the names she called her. And she was not too partial to me or our Alfie either. She got on well with her other daughters-in-law, though – or so it seemed. But what we knew for sure was that she liked the other grandchildren, but not us.

We travelled with the old grandparents when we were young, but me Dad always pulled up the road aways from Grandad's wagon, so that the two women couldn't bicker – and each would take a different road to hawk the doors. Whatever the old Granny got while out calling, we chavvies saw nothing of it. We knew she got things, because she was good at begging and bartering – she could beg the hind legs off a donkey – yet it wasn't us she begged for but her other grandchildren. She had dozens of grandchildren by her sons and daughter – not that we begrudged them the clothes or shoes because we chavvies all got on well together. It was the sly way she would do things. She would tuck the begged things away in her wagon and then make a big show of handing them out when we met up with one or other of me Dad's brothers. We got used to this kind of treatment from the old woman. Me Mam and Dad would tell us to take it with a pinch of salt, for what we needed they would provide.

It's a pity we couldn't stop up the Lane, because I liked the place very much. It had two entrances, one at the top and one at the bottom, it was quite wide in places and it was kushti to play there and pick the wild flowers. It was like a safe haven. No one apart from the farmer who shared the track to get to his fields had any rights up there; it was a privately owned stopping tan (place). No strangers could enter our stopping place for me Grandad had bought it years afore. He owned it along with another Traveller called Johnny Ayres. It was a safe place to leave us, if the grown-ups went out hawking. But the old Granny made it impossible for me Dad's little family to enjoy any of it.

With hugs and kisses from me Grandad, we left the Lane. The old gal stayed in her hut so we never set yocks on her, thank goodness, or me Mam and Dad would have ended up at loggerheads. There was really no sound reason why the old Granny never took to or liked me Mam, but her capers made me Mam really turn on her and she would tell me Dad what she thought of his old mother.

'Your old mother, my Len, is a bloody old cow, and one of these days I'll ferget her age and put her on her back.'

'That will do you a fat lot of good, my Vie. You won't win no medals by doing that to a woman twice your age, my old gal.'

'Twice me age or not she's asking for it – and I don't like the way she treats my chavvies. What have they ever done to the old bitch?'

'Nothing, my Vie.'

'Well, my chavvies is as good as any of her other grand-chavvies – no better and no worse.'

'My Vie, I knows that, but me Mum must have been dropped on her head when she was born, so give over now. If we two falls out over her, then we makes her happy.'

'I'll make her happy one of these days, my Len, if I dicks her near a pond, I'll shove her in on her head.'

'You wouldn't, my Vie.'

'Oh yes I would – and dare anybody to pull her out.'

Luckily they both burst out laughing, which was a good sign that this time at least there would be no rows over the old Granny and her antics.

At the bottom of Dunkerton Hill we came upon a wagon with a broken wheel. It turned out to be Kalub and Sistery, members of the old White family, who travels up from time to time from Dorset, just as we travels down to their area. So we all knows each other well.

'You got a bit of trouble, brother,' said me Dad.

'I have that,' Kalub answered. 'Me bloody wheel went.'

'Better here than on one of they tight bends,' laughed me Dad, pulling off the road to give a hand.

Walking back to the broken-down wagon, me Dad told Kalub he knew of a farmer who just might sell him a wheel that would fit the wagon, and they went off to see.

Sistery and me Mam got together for a catch up.

'I got me a baby, my Fiance,' said Sistery. 'It's a little boy. He's up in the wagon in the warm.'

'How old is he?' me Mam wanted to know.

'About four months.'

'I'll have to find him something. Hang on.' And off me Mam went.

It's a Gypsy custom that each new baby be given a little bit of vonger (money) as a kushti luck charm. Back she come with a couple of sixpenny pieces.

'Here, put this in his little hand and let him hold it for a few seconds.'

'Oh, I will at that, my Fiance. Thank you very much.'

It took some little while but when the men came back they were rolling a wheel a-tween them.

'Let's hope it fits, my brother,' laughed Kalub.

Funny, all our men called each other 'brother' even though there was no bloodline.

The wheel fitted and we all set off up the steep hill together.

'You get in front of me, Kalub, then I gins where yum at.'

We chavvies and me Mam and Sistery walked on behind, Sistery carrying her baby in a tight bundle to keep it warm. We would catch up to the wagon each time they stopped to let the grys get their breath back, afore kicking off again till they reached the top. This was a long hill and they did it in stops and starts – with our Alfie close at hand with the drag shoe to block the back wheels each time they stopped so that the wagon didn't roll backwards. A drag shoe or wind-up brake to assist the horses when going up and down hills was a must. The drag shoe was put in front or behind a back wheel when going up or down steep hills to hold the wagon back: it would handicap the wheel, taking some of the strain and weight off the horse. Sometimes the molly block which we used to make the wooden clothes pegs on doubled up as a drag shoe. The molly block was always kept close at hand when travelling, to be used in an emergency. Because the drag shoe hung on a chain beneath the side of the wagon, it was quicker to use the molly block if need be.

Kalub ran his back wheel into the kerb – it was the only thing he could do to help his gry get a start when he pulled on again. These wagons were dead weights on steep inclines.

Once up the hill we parted company. Kalub was going to the blacksmith's shop to have his wheels checked, afore heading where his mind took him. Handshaking over, we hollered our farewells and went on our way.

When we hit Bath we went under the train line, then over the river bridge, right in among the shops and out the other side – where we waited for me Mam who had gone off to do a bit of calling in the shops she knew. Bath is a big old town, but quite friendly towards us. While we were waiting both our two grys made a mess in the road, but it was not there for long. Out come buckets and shovels – 'Good stuff for the roses,' these men would laugh as they nearly came to blows over who got the most. Me Dad said we should have charged tuppence a bucket, then they wouldn't have been so quick to play with hoss dung.

At last we could shift on, all riding in the wagon, and we pulled on to the outskirts of Bath for the night. We could have carried on to Chapel Plaister, but our grys had already dragged the wagon up one long hill today. That was enough for one day's work, Dad told us. Although young, Alfie and me knew these roads well – and we also knew that a few more miles would bring us to the common. We longed to reach it for once on this little common we would be out of reach of the law moving us on and could stay for months if needs be. To top it off, there was sure to be other families taking a break there and that meant other chavvies to play with and to go with us to fetch wood and water.

It was still bitterly cold weather, but we were hardened to it. It made no difference if it rained or blowed so long as we were all together and could make a yog to warm and cook by. Many a time some lady would fire at me Mam that we two were suffering with the cold or rain – they liked to poke their noses in our business.

'You look after yourself, Missus, and I'll look after mine,' was the normal answer given.

'You should be reported for keeping little children out in all weathers,' one dear soul told me Mam. Little did this person know me Mam or Dad could never keep us two shut up in the wagon: we wanted to be out in the open with them. Out we got and stayed out. Gorgies did not understand our way of life – we are outdoor people, hardened to what the weather throws at us, and we deal with it in our own way.

Me Dad, by the talk we heard, was expecting our mare to have a foal this year. We two were never involved in this kind of grown-up talk – we often wondered why. It was years later when we were growing up that we found out it took 'two to tangle', as we used to say. But for now it was yet another one of their secrets, to be kept from young minds. We had no idea where puppies, foals or babies come from – and that's how all Romanies wanted it. What they wanted for all chavvies was a carefree, clear-minded childhood, a 'clean life', as they put it, trouble free. And I can honestly say we had that, all eight of us chavvies, which was the number of chavvies me Mam and Dad ended up with

Aunt Dhinea Isaacs, in her eighties and still step-dancing, at a Gypsy History Month gathering.

altogether. We were eventually eight little chicks, as me Dad used to call us, but for now they only had we three, me and our Alfie and little Jess.

We pulled onto the common early next morning and found quite a few families already settled in. Rubin and Brit, Andrew and Dhinea, me Dad's brother Jessie and his wife Louie, and a few members of the old White and Hughes families.

We had a grand few weeks on the common. No problems, every family feeling happy, awaiting the time to head back down country for the pea season. And to top it all, we might travel with some of them, which was kushti news for me and our Alfie and Jess.

How we looked forward to the summer months and pea season.

The clothes and bedding were turned out the wagons so they could be spring-cleaned. And the men got their paintbrushes out to touch up the outside of the wagons. They would have to look smart in front of the hundreds of other Travellers who would be in the pea country, as they called it, which was around Bridgwater. As there was several pea and broad-bean growers, there would be plenty of work to be had.

So, on a morning in the middle of May, the wagons slowly rolled off the common and headed back towards Bath. As we came down Box Hill, we got our first full view of the line of wagons and carts plus a few trolleys. We could hear the sound of dozens of horseshoes hitting the hard surface of the road, clip-clopping in convoy towards the city of Bath.

As we were one of the last lot to pull out, we could see the wagons from the top of the hill making their way down. It was a grand sight, I can tell you. We were holding up the traffic and word ran forward to pull in and break up into smaller groups – otherwise the Bath police would surely do it for us. We are not too popular in the eyes of the Law; even when we're on the move they still harass us at every opportunity. And at times our men will travel together to give them something to really shout about.

In Bath in the Fifties town the police had big black cars to drive around in, so they could get around at top speed, unlike the village gavvers who only had pushbikes to catch us up on. Bath is a lovely town, full to the brim with shops of every kind. As the wagons entered one of the main streets we came to a sudden stop, having caught up to the rest of the convoy. We had two routes we could use to travel through Bath, one followed the river with a good road in and out of the town whilst the other took us right through the middle. It was the second one we chose on this day, the one we normally avoided, for the streets were narrow and lined on either side with shops and pubs.

'What's up now?' voiced me Dad to his brother Jessie in front. 'Sounds to me like somebody been run over,' he answers. 'I'll go and take a shufti.' Then we heard Jessie calling to me Dad, 'Come yer, our Lenard, and take a dick at this caper.'

Giving the driving reins to me Mam, off went me Dad. It turned out a row of police had blocked off the road and wouldn't let the wagons go through the town. It was a big mistake on their part because the roads in Bath are not wide enough to turn round a horse pulling a wagon. There was only one way to sort it out and that was by going ahead, but they gavvers was having none of it. The police had made a stand to show us we could not do as we liked in their town: 'Turn about and take the other road. You're not coming through here.'

A crowd began to gather and watch the fun. It got bigger as word spread through the town of trouble brewing between a gang of Gypsies and the law. Our grys was getting restless what with people walking under their heads to get a better view or just crossing the road between the wagons.

'Back up, my Len, get our gry out of this. She's sweating up and her heavy in foal,' called me Mam.

'My Vie, the tober's blocked behind us with cars and lorries. If I tries to turn round, out goes the shop winders – which we would have to pay for. We ain't got that kind of vonger, any road.'

'Well hold these bloody reins while I tells they gavvers a thing or two,' and with that she jumps off the foreboard and is off, pushing her way up front.

'Alfie, Maggie, dick after the gry. I gotta ketch your Mam afore she gets six months.'

'You dick after the gry, our Alfie,' and off I pushes to follow me Dad – I wants to dick for meself the goings-on. I gets there just in time to hear me Mam saying, 'We can't turn back and the horses is upset. If one rears up then the rest will rear and buck, and people will get trodden on and killed stone dead. Now let us through, you bastard of a mush, you done this on purpose.'

The policeman ignored me Mam but another was making his way to her and he looked like he meant business.

'You'm all the same, you lot,' shouted me Mam, as this gavver made a grab for her. Me Dad and Uncle Jessie jumped in front of her to protect her. Jessie's shirt flew off as did me Dad's and a dozen or so of our men and boys did the same. Dad shouted, 'If you lays one hand on our women and chavvies, you have to fight we men. Police or no police, we've had enough of yis lot.'

Me Mam had brought things to a head, and with a bunch of very angry Gypsy men ready and willing to fight for their women, chavvies, horses and wagons, they must have looked a fearsome sight.

Then a head gavver mush appeared and tried to calm things down. But even the gorgie bystanders could see it was the Law causing the problems and told them so. 'Let the Gypsies through and get the street cleared. We got our businesses to think of.'

The head mush had seen now who was at the root of the trouble: his own officers. This was a main road for everyone to use; they had no right to block us out. And two hours of our day had already been wasted – horses so worked up that they dropped dollops of dung in the road and their hot pee ran in puddles. It was a right old mess. And smelled a bit too.

We had never in our lives been hand-clapped on our way, but now the crowds did so with smiles and cheers. I think our people had chosen this route on purpose that day – to show the Law we could pass through this town like anybody else. The Law had been turning wagons back from going through the town but for once we had enough wagons together to make a show of force. But it could have ended badly. This episode was laughed about long after, but it was not so funny at the time. Lives could easily have been lost, with so many people about and given the narrowness of the road.

It took a while for tempers to run down and for us to find a place to pull in and chat about what had happened. Me Mam was proper fightable and could have ended up in jail. Also, most of the wagons were full of little chavvies who could have been maimed if any of the horses had kicked off. This was all very worrying. Would other towns follow the Bath gavvers and try to stop us passing through? I'm glad to say this never did happen. But over the years the police did everything they could to stop us travelling and, at the same time, to stop us from *stopping*. It made no sense to us at all.

When we pulled off the roads, onto the pea field and out of the gavvers' sight, it was sheer bliss. We had a really kushti season and kushti weather to help us as well. As the shillings piled up, we got ourselves spruced up for the Bridgwater Fair, which I'll be coming back to later on.

Chapter Four

Near Death Experience

T HINKING ABOUT WHAT COULD HAVE HAPPENED to our children in the wagons in Bath has brought back the memory of an accident that happened to me as a child. It was of me own making and it left me with a legacy I dearly wish I did not have.

It was around 1944, and the war was still raging, when me Dad decided to pull onto Melksham Common in the county of Wiltshire. We had been travelling on our own for months, for various reasons, including the safety of us chavvies: at times we would come across a family whose chavvies were spiteful and who would hurt us younger ones. Then our dads would take up with their dads and there would be fights. Another reason for travelling alone was that it was easier to earn a living that way. But we was getting fed up with our own company, so it was decided to share a few weeks with others on the Common and catch up with everyone's news.

Me and our Alfie got the usual dire warnings of what not to do, which cleared from me brain the minute the wagon rolled to a stop on the pretty little common and I spied all the chavvies running and playing free as birds. It was a sight I hadn't seen in months and I wanted some of that shared freedom and them Traveller chavvies to play with. I knew most of them on sight and they in turn called me and welcomed me into their midst.

I was young, only three or four years old, but older than my years as we chavvies were wont to be. I knew right from wrong: I had strict parents who worried about me and cared for me. But that day I ran about like a dinalow (fool). For company I had girls who was as daft as meself and full of fun. We were let loose to play and it was exciting. I played so much I must have got thirsty and wanted to fill up with water so I could carry on the game. In my haste to get a drink I broke every warning me Mam and Dad had ever given me: I ran right past the chrome water-can that was full of fresh clean water (which I would've known). Instead I ran full pelt to the yog, where I had spied the big black iron kettle. I stooped down and put me mouth to the spout and drank and swallowed – then screamed me head off. I had drunk boiling water.

I remember me Mam screaming too. I was bundled in someone's arms and ridden on horseback to the doctor who sent me straight to the hospital with the life choking out of me.

The water I had swallowed was causing blisters to form in me throat and they were choking me. Me parents were told not to hold out much hope. As I have little or no memory of all this, I can only relate what my parents have told me. I lay in the hospital for several days, my life hanging by a thread. Desperately worried about their other chavvies, who had been left on the Common to be cared for and fed by the other families, my parents decided to slip back and check up on them. They told the hospital they would not be gone long.

On reaching the Common they were surrounded by the others, all asking if I was alive or dead, when an old woman pushed her way through the group towards me Mam.

'Outta me road, yis lot, get outta me way,' she told them. 'I wants to speak to the little body,' as she referred to me Mam. 'Young umman,' she said ('umman' was how she pronounced 'woman'), 'Come to me a minute and listen to what I have to say. You got bad trouble on your hands, young umman.' This was a statement made with deep feeling on the old woman's part.

'Yes, my Aunt, I got real bad trouble. It looks like I'm gonna lose me little gal.' (We call older people 'Aunt' or 'Uncle' to show respect.)

'Well hear me out,' answered the old woman. 'If you gives me a pair of pretty plates and a bar of soap, you just might have yourself some kushti news.'

Apparently me Mam pushed the old woman away and laughed and cried at the same time. 'Don't yis think I got enough on me hands without you, my Aunt? Take everything I got. If I loses me gal I shan't want nothing...'

Off went the old woman, heading back to her old wagon. Me Mam was shook and twisted around all shapes by the other women: 'My Fiance, go and say you're sorry to that old gal, fer God's sake ... She can do more harm than good to you ... Quick, catch her up ... my Fiance, that old gal is a gub and well-known for it...' (A gub is someone who can put a curse on you and not to be underestimated.)

'What?' cried me Mam, 'Why didn't yis lot warn me? Oh my God, what have I done?' And she pushed off from the group and ran after the old woman.

'Please, my Aunt, please, wait a minute,' she cried to the old woman.

She stopped and turned on me Mam. 'Young umman, you take your road and I'll take mine'.

'I'm begging yis to hear me out. *Please* hear me out. I'm not from this part of the country, I don't know your ways. Please, my Aunt, if you can help me, you can have me own life – anything I got, which ain't much.'

'Yis laughed at me.' The old woman was shaking.

'Laugh, my Aunt? I ain't got a laugh left in me body. Me baby's dying in the hospital. It's me nerves, not laughing you heard.'

'Alright, young umman, I'll help you. You'm young and foolish and

33

would laugh if yer granny's arse catched fire. But hear me out: never laugh at what yis knows nothing about. There's things in this life bigger than all of us, so take heed of me. Now give me a pair of your pretty plates and a bar of soap.'

'Come and take what you want, my Aunt,' begged me Mam.

'I'll only take what I asked for from you – nothing more, nothing less.'

Together they walked back to our wagon. There me Mam opened up her hamper and pulled out her pretty plates, but could only find a sliver of soap to hand over.

'Do yis part with these things with a good heart or do yis begrudge giving um, young umman?'

'With a good heart, my Aunt. I swear with a good heart and thank you from the bottom of me heart.'

'Well, get yisselves back to the hospital, then. The little chavvie needs her Mam an' Dad. So get going and don't waste me time.'

As they neared the hospital they met a gavver on horseback who told them the doctor wanted to see them. He had been sent to fetch them back to the hospital. A lot of police still rode horses in the Forties. Thinking I had died, they entered the hospital cursing themselves for leaving me when they did.

'We only been gone an hour or less,' cried me Dad, 'and left our baby gal to die alone,' so sure were they that I had gone.

'I shan't ever forgive meself,' wept me Mam.

'And nor will I,' sniffed me Dad. It's not acceptable in our community to let a loved one die alone.

So, with tears freely falling, they went to the ward I was in, expecting the worse, only to be met by a smiling doctor.

'Good news,' he said, 'We've managed to stop the blisters forming in her throat. If we can continue like this she should be fine – still very ill but she'll recover.'

'What happened, doctor?' asked me Dad. 'Because only a few hours ago you told us there was no hope for my little gal.'

'Well I'm not sure myself,' answered the doctor mush. 'I really don't know how this change came about. It seems we've stopped the blisters forming with little sips of a mixture we've made up for her. A nurse has been giving it to her. But I must say that if, after you left the hospital, you prayed for a miracle like I know you Gypsies do, then the Good Lord must have heard you...'

(Another doctor said these very same words to me many years later when me Dad had been diagnosed with cancer and given only a certain time to live. I had been shown me Dad's x-rays and had the lung cancer pointed out to me. But the time limit the doctor put on me Dad came and went. In fact two years passed until one day we called the doctor out to see to me Mam. I took the opportunity to ask him about me Dad's cancer and he said, 'You're a Gypsy family and if you prayed for a miracle you got one.' Me Dad no longer had cancer and he lived another ten years. Either he had been wrongly diagnosed or our prayers worked.)

The doctor looking after me and my scalded throat was a little mystified, but me Mam and Dad knew instantly what they had to thank for the turnaround: a pair of pretty plates and a sliver of soap ... and that wonderful old gub. The one-in-a-million who was camped on that common when me parents was in dire trouble. When they got back to the common that day they rushed to thank her but she had packed up and left while they were with me.

'Where is she?' Dad asked. 'Where's that old gal? I wants to see her.'

'You won't see her, my brother,' one of the men told him, 'she's long gone by now.' Which was exactly the same as me Mam was being told by the womenfolk: 'She's long gone, my Fiance.'

'But why? I wanted to speak to her. I've got to speak to her. I shan't be happy till I speak to her.'

'Well, just thank your lucky stars you even met her, my Fiance. I doubt you'll see her again,' me Mam was told.

'But why didn't she wait for us to come back and tell her what had happened to me little gal?'

'Because, my dear Aunt Fiance, she already knowed what happened. Just you listen to us lot for a minute. She pulled on this common just after you did – like she knowed she would be wanted or needed. Then, when she spoke to you she packed up and went, she pulled out right after you went back to the hospital. Now *you* may not know her, but we upcountry Travellers do – she's a person only God knows how old, but that woman is a pure gub. If anybody does anything to upset her, she will put the scuss on 'em. On the other hand, she loves little chavvies and has always got a sweet or two to hand out. She travels on her own and bothers nobody. Her name is Lyzzer, or Aunt Lyzzer, she's as clean as a smelt and keeps herself by fortune-telling. They do reckon her old gry and juckle (dog) are as old as she is herself. But one thing's for sure, nobody messes with her.'

A few years later old Lyzzer was found dead in her wagon by the roadside. If only I had asked me Mam and Dad where she was buried, I would visit her graveside and lay flowers. All I remember is that the Travellers gave her a kushti funeral, which she paid for herself, having left vonger hidden in her wagon.

This episode was added to our fireside tales and repeated many times, so without knowing it for years I was part of our Gypsy history as told round the yog. But God love that woman, she left me a part of herself I could do without – because (and I'm not a bit proud to own up to this) I am like her: I can put the scuss on people. I have done it in a hot temper, and it has fruited.

The gift, or should I say curse, can be passed on by someone who saves your life, as happened to me. It's an awful burden to have, especially with my hot temperament. As a Gypsy, people not of my race quite often say to me (joking) that I should put a curse on someone. I smile to meself and think, 'If only you knew who you're joking with.' I don't want to go through life with people fearing me – quite the opposite: I want to help people as can't help themselves. I believe that's my life's role. But I know to this day that, if I let her, Old Lyzzer would live on through me. Nor can I stop others that she helped (and according to the old tales it was many), so out there in my community there are gubs...

Yet I made my beloved husband a promise years ago that I would not curse another person – and so far I have succeeded. I will not lay any more curses on anyone, no matter how much they upset me. Me Dad had a saying, 'If yis can't do no good, then do no harm.'

Me brother Robert was a witness to some of the bad things I did in the past, one or two of which I did intend to do. He never found it funny when a curse of mine fruited. It amazed him but he would say, 'I don't like this, it's dead spooky.' He'd be happy to know I don't lay curses any more.

Chapter Five

Our Beginnings

I BELIEVE MY GYPSY RACE TO BE UNIQUE. I write 'unique' because when you have read our history (or as much as I can relate here) and you discover that after all these years we are still here to tell the tale, I truly believe you'll agree it is unique: simply because of our history, in particular those dark centuries when my people were put to death or sold into slavery – not because they had committed any crimes, but simply because they were born into a community known as Gypsies.

Our fight for survival in these lands started from the very day back in the late fourteenth century when a group of Gypsies first arrived on the shores of Scotland. And so our history in Britain began. It's a long, dark history thanks to the expulsions, executions and even enslavement that were brought down on our community thanks to orders and bills and acts of Parliament made by the rulers of Britain down the centuries. (I cannot be absolutely certain of all the facts in this chapter as there is so little in the records, so if I'm out by a year or two, forgive an old Gypsy woman.)

Our history has to be told, not only to the settled community, but to we Romanies as well – my race should know of their ancestors and what happened to them. That history has made us what we are today. I confess, I never knew much of what our families went through down through the years until I read about the few records there are. I remember bits of old tales told by the elders while we sat round our fires at night, bits that had been handed down through the generations, that had become faded with time – as with everything else, the older the tale the more unbelievable it becomes. Little did me Dad and others know, back then, that me Grandad was not rambling in his mind: he was remembering fragments his Dad and his Grandad had told him, about hangings and murders committed against members of their families.

If we had been able to write down the details of actual deaths and how and why they happened, we could have had a fuller picture of the events that took place, but alas it was not to be. The Gypsies of old used the only way they knew and that was to bind the things that happened to them in old fireside tales, believing that that way they would not be lost or forgotten. But as the generations succeeded each other and life got better for our community, these tales did gradually get lost.

We can't rely on the old fireside tales for our history any more. Today's Gypsy communities can learn of the dark deeds done to a race who had no one to protect them by reading accounts that have been pieced together by scholars – both Gypsy and non-Gypsy. There's a list at the end of this book of Romani history books which will tell you more of what little is known. But we don't have a complete picture because so few records survived.

What I can do, though, is let my imagination take me back to those early times. Even if I don't know the exact details of what happened to my ancestors, I can picture in my mind how it must have been for them.

Imagine the first Travellers who arrived on these shores, by boat. We don't know much about why they came or exactly where they came from, but at this time and going back around a century, Gypsies were spreading out through Europe – through Germany, France, Switzerland, Belgium, Holland, Italy, Spain, Russia, Sweden and Denmark. They were mostly coming from Byzantium in the East. Perhaps it was the Black Death that drove them westwards, perhaps it was persecution or war. They were nomads and it was in their blood to travel.

When they first arrived they probably wouldn't have been understood by the local people. Maybe that was why they were reported to the authorities, because people were suspicious of the strangers. The newcomers would have stood out from the peasants and been noticed, if only for the way they were dressed and their darker skin and hair.

They would not have been able to communicate because they spoke in their own language. They would have been looked upon with distrust. Many times they must have been asked, 'Where do you come from? Who are you?' and the lack of communication must have been very frustrating for both sides. I suppose they must have been able to get some sort of work to enable them to survive and gradually the language barriers must have broken down too as the Travellers picked up the local way of talking. But they would not have starved – they would have caught plenty of wildlife such as pheasant or rabbit to cook and found a fresh stream for drinking water. They handed the ways and means of surviving down through our generations.

Working alongside the locals, their workmanship would have been noticed. Their special skills in metalworking perhaps came in useful. They would have held their own in that capacity: hard work would have been second nature to them. And even if they could now speak the local lingo, they would have hung on to their own Romani language along with their culture and customs. These they would not give up. But years would pass, children would have been born and bred so the numbers of the Gypsies were growing. Being nomads, small groups would have broken away from the mother group and worked their way down to English soil – family units that would have stuck closely together: that's our way of life, always seeking work and new pastures to do it in.

Little groups would have thought they would be less likely to get noticed – how wrong they were. In 1530 that murderous swine of a king, Henry VIII (to my mind the instigator of the very problems we have today) passed the 'Egyptians Act' through Parliament. It made it the law to expel the 'outlandish people calling themselves Egyptians', meaning Gypsies (the name itself being a corrupted version of 'Egyptians' – people believed the Gypsies had come from 'Little Egypt' an area in Greece which was easily confused with Egypt itself). This Act accused Gypsies of 'deceiving people' by telling fortunes and also of committing robbery. No more Gypsies were allowed to enter the country and those already in England had sixteen days' notice to leave. The Gypsies would have been mere sport to a king who would go on to have two of his wives put to death.

Once word of this new law became known to the little pockets of Gypsies, in my mind's eye I see them taking to the woods and forests to hide. This would not have been too hard for them – they could survive for years like that, living off the wildlife and fish. The country would have been mostly wild and uncultivated back then, easy to get lost in if needs be. If they were ill, they would have made their own medicines and potions – the very medicines and potions we were still making and using many generations later, for they were passed down by word of mouth. Every bit of knowledge and skill was passed on from person to person and is still in use today. But by the same token, the prejudice was also handed down from generation to generation. In Henry VIII's time children were told not to play or have anything to do with Gypsy children. You would not believe it, but parents still tell their children not to play with our children today – almost five hundred years later. That's how things get handed down from one generation to the next.

In Scotland, around the year 1492, King James IV gave some Gypsy leaders special powers to use their own laws and justice system to govern their own people. The King seems to have given special protection to some Gypsy families who were in his favour, but not to others. And in fact as the years went on, just as was happening in England and other countries, more and more rules and regulations came in to restrict Gypsies' freedoms. Governments wanted nothing more than to eradicate Gypsies from their countries.

So the Gypsies continued to live a hidden life. Down in England, in 1554, during the reign of Queen Mary (better known as 'Bloody Mary', an apt name for such a human being) a new Egyptians Act was passed, a disaster as far as our people were concerned – all Gypsies and anyone found associating with them would be put to death. Being a Gypsy meself, I know that those Gypsies would have taken any steps they could to save their families. There was no one but themselves left to trust. And they must have survived, otherwise I would not be here today and nor would many of my race.

We are still looked upon with suspicion today, and this is the reason why we Romanies like to keep ourselves to ourselves. Over the years we've guarded our culture and customs – and even more so our language – which is all we have left from those earlier generations.

Now, as I think back, when we travelled with Grandad Dannal all those years ago, we probably retraced the journeys of our people who were being chased away or hunted down, because me Grandad would have been following the roads and lanes *his* great Grandad had travelled with *his* Grandad – and here he was, showing his sons and grandchildren those very same routes.

As a child I well remember that me Dad and other Travellers had by-lanes or commons they would head for, to pull in and get a few days' peace from being hunted on by the police. Now I wonder if our ancestors used these same hiding places to escape from the laws of the day. I have no doubt they did – and that we travelled in their footprints. That gives you an idea how old our stopping places really are: generation after generation stopped in the very same places. Even with today's motorway system, most of the old byways and lanes remain. The stopping places are still there but fenced off to prevent our using them – but we still likes to travel back to them and reminisce about days gone by.

I also remember that when we were pulled on these out-of-the-way places, we were highly tuned in to the behaviour of our horses and dogs and even the wildlife. By keeping a yock and an ear on these animals, we could get an early warning that someone was afoot – that we were about to get a visitor. The horses would stop munching grass and lift up their heads to listen, then prick up their ears, neigh or whinny a warning – and look in the direction of interest. Dogs would stand up at a stance, which we knew well was a warning: the hair round their necks would bristle up, head cocked to one side listening, afore they barked their warning. Birds would suddenly fly from hedges and trees – animals and birds have keener hearing and eyesight than we do – and a better sense of smell. It was primitive but we made full use of it.

That was how our ancestors would have known someone was coming near their camps. It's second nature for us to know all these things. In fact we know so many things we don't even realise other people never thinks of them. And all this knowledge would have been used in them foregone terrible times.

In 1573, back in Scotland, the Gypsies were ordered by law to stop travelling and settle down. If they gave up their nomadic way of life then they would be accepted into the community. Those that did not would be expelled from the country. Was it ever going to end, they must have thought? I could answer that one for them. No, my dear long-dead relatives, it would not end, for here I am in 2012 and the aim of the government today is to force us to settle down. It's a way of weakening our identity, for our race to become diluted and lost within the settled community. This will never happen, because we are what we are, we're Gypsies.

In the twentieth century, when the Gypsies had been in Europe for over five hundred years and were still maintaining our way of life in spite of the best efforts of so many to stamp us out, there came Hitler and his

Holocaust. Gypsies and Sinti from many countries where the Nazis had taken power were rounded up and sent to camps such as Auschwitz, Bergen-Belsen, Buchenwald and Dachau. Hitler and his henchmen murdered hundreds of thousands of our people in ways so terrible it's almost impossible to imagine, but imagine it I do, and it breaks me heart.

Each year I light a candle in church in memory of all our people murdered in the Holocaust during those dark unforgettable years. What happened must never be forgotten – we cannot let it happen again.

I have never been able to cross water – it's part of what makes me a Gypsy – and because of that I've never held a passport. I believe, like me, most of our older generation won't cross water, but the younger generation have got over this and are able to fly in planes – that's one way we have had to change over the years. So I have never visited these terrible camps where my people were murdered. But, this coming year, I'm going to get my first ever passport and some friends of mine are going to help me go through the Channel Tunnel so that I can visit Auschwitz. As I say, it's against my beliefs to cross water or go under water (where the birds don't fly or sing) but I will do it. I have a deep need to do this and I'm prepared to break a lifetime of never travelling overseas: I need to pay my respects to the people we lost in the Holocaust.

When the Holocaust was going on, we had no idea our people were living and dying in other countries. At that time, going about our daily lives, we thought we were the only Gypsies. And those poor people over in Europe probably never knew we existed either. So uneducated were we that other countries did not touch on our lives or, if they did, it meant nothing to us. Our world was where we were and where we travelled to, to pull in for a few days or weeks. Nothing existed apart from that – our horizons stretched no further than the areas we already knew, which is hard to believe today, but back then that was our world and it was as though there was nothing beyond it.

This is one of the reasons our community stuck together, and why we'd get excited if we met others like ourselves from different parts of the country. Our lives were very secluded and separate from the gorgie population. That's how we were able to continue our way of life over so many centuries. Even now I find it hard to believe how we have progressed in just a few short years: never in me dreams when I was young did I think I would one day be able to drive a car – that was not for us, that was gorgie life. We had no ambitions – only to carry on our old ways, which had been handed down through the generations. We had to guard them closely and preserve them so that they might continue.

Travel and education have brought us to where we are today. I remember when I used to pick hops, I'd hear the people that had come down from London and other big towns talking to each other, about their lives there – I never knew and neither did me Dad which direction London was. That's how small our world was. Oh yes, we had heard about these places on our old wireless set but we had no idea where they were or what they were like.

Recently I saw the Tower of London for the first time and was disappointed at how low it was. I had thought it would tower right up in the air. In me mind, those towns I heard talk of years ago were huge. To me a big town was Bath or Bridgwater, Wells or Bristol. In those days we could take the wagons right through the middle of those places and stop in the main streets to shop or hawk our swag. I don't think wagons and horses would be as welcome today on their high streets, but it would be a grand sight.

If ever a race of people have suffered for being different my lot have and still are. It's not hanging or slavery or mass murder we have to live with now, it's the lack of somewhere to live, lack of healthcare and access to appropriate education. We need these things to give our babies, young and elderly a decent quality of life.

And because of all that went on before, anyone in authority is still feared and distrusted by us Romani Gypsies today. As an activist I have worked with the police for many years to educate them on Gypsy cultural issues, but when I'm driving my old car, if a police officer is driving behind me, the hairs on the back of me neck goes stiff and sticks up for no good reason. I know I haven't committed an offence, but it makes no difference. Many of my community tell me the same thing happens to them – it's a sick feeling of fear. The word 'authority' sets alarm bells ringing for us Gypsies and we think, 'What do they want now? I've done nothing...' It's said this happens if you're a criminal, but most of us are not criminals and it still happens.

Chapter Six

A Change of Lifestyle

W E GYPSIES SURVIVED THE WAR YEARS, hiding in lanes and back roads. Many of our men and boys got took to fight and many never came back. After the War, life gradually got back to a normal routine as we travelled in and around our old, familiar areas. The men and boys that had survived the War returned and went back to their travelling areas in search of their families. Some were never the same again, they came back with limbs missing or shell shocked but they were all welcomed back by their loving families: mothers and fathers and wives who had no idea if their sons or husbands had survived or been killed, because being Travellers travelling the roads they had no address to which information could be sent to them. Some parents died while they were waiting and hoping for their loved ones to return.

As for the ones that did make it back, life was never the same for them. They found it hard to settle and to cope with life. I know that one of me Mam's relations that came back shell shocked took his own life. I will not name this blessed man because his sons and daughters are still with us today; it would only open old wounds and bring them pain.

So life went on. We continued to work the land and lots of families like mine collected scrap metals and rags round the house-dwellers' doors or bred horses to sell on at fairs or to anyone looking for a good working horse. We chavvies were growing up with a dad taking the reins again, not that he had been sent abroad to fight. He spent most of the War in and around Bristol fire-fighting (taking off every so often to look for us, his little family, to check we were still alive, because he knew we could have been bombed, stopping as we were in the lanes on the outskirts of Bristol).

Then something occurred that has stayed with me ever since. I don't know the exact year this happened – dates and times meant nothing to us in those days – only that it was some time in the 1950s. But what I remember clearly is how very afraid my people were.

We had been up round Wiltshire doing a few farm jobs and decided to pull back onto Chapel Plaister common. We had pulled as normal on a free part of the common and were pleased to see a few other families stopping there on both sides of the little narrow lane that split the common in half. I well remember the weather was fine and warm and the smell of smoke from cooking yogs filled the air – meat suet puddings were bubbling away in the big old black pots and the cabbage boiling (my lot loved cabbage).

We soon unpacked and settled in. As they did every day, all the men went off dropping rag bills or to do their chosen work. The women, meanwhile, stayed on the common cooking and washing or just sitting by the yog having a chat. Little knowing that once again the government was planning another move against us. It was well planned and intended, in the long run, to deal with us once and for all. Like newborn babies we sat on that common, not knowing our freedom was in the balance.

On this day we chavvies was running around the common collecting wood and water and playing as we went – having a grand old time. Our mams were doing whatever came to hand (all the men long gone since early morning, earning their living) when a strange black official-looking car pulled in on the common and parked some distance from the scattered wagons. Two men got out.

'Gavvers!' went up the cry, warning the others that the police was here.

'That's not gavvers,' cried one, 'I don't gin [know] who they mushes is' (the gavvers always wore a uniform, unlike these men).

'What do you want?' asked one of the older women as the two mushes got closer to the tight bunch of women that had now formed.

'We want to talk to you,' said one, holding up a piece of paper.

'What about?' the old gal asked again.

'We're here to help you people.'

'We don't need no help,' said the old gal, who was to be the spokesperson. 'None of your kind of help, I'll warrant.'

'You may as well hear me out. It's for your own good.'

'Look, mate, get yourself away and come back when our men's here. We shan't be talking to you about nothing. There's no men allowed round our wagons when our own men is not here. Now get yourselves off out of it.'

'No,' says this mush, spreading his feet to show who was boss. 'Gather round. I'm only going to tell you this once.' His voice was rising and he called the other mush over to him, to back him up.

There was a real sense of unease on the common now.

'My Lenard's never about when he's needed,' grumbled me Mam. Some of the other women said the same of their husbands.

'If you starts to talk dirty talk, then we women will beat you off the common,' stated the old gal. 'We shan't have no dirty talk here.' This was just a way to try to get the upper hand when their men were not with them. Fear of the unknown was always the worst thing.

'This is about your future,' said the mush, 'I'm not going to "talk dirty talk", as you put it.'

'Then spit it out and be gone.'

'We're going to build you people camps to live on. You will stop travelling the highways and move onto these camps.'

'CAMPS! You is going to put we people on camps? – you expect us to live on camps? What camps – tell us that much, what camps?'

Keep in mind that they had all heard the word 'camps' on the wireless – meaning concentration camps. Everyone was speaking or shouting at once now. The word 'camp' had fired all the women up.

'These camps,' the second mush now shouted, 'will be built out in the countryside. You can take your wagons onto the camps to live in, so you can keep what you've got.'

'We shan't go onto no camps!' You can't force us to live on no camps was the gist of what they was telling the two mushes.

'Oh yes you will. We haven't finished telling you the alternative. If you don't stop all this travelling and go on the camps to live, we will take your children and put them into care in order to get them educated. These children must be educated.'

Oh doughty, oh dear old doughty (oh dear, oh dear), the women went mad. One picked up a long burning ember from the yog – if the mush hadn't took to his heels, he would have been made to swallow it. Both mushes made it back to their car and drove off, leaving devastated women and shaking children in their wake.

Anyone can threaten the grown-ups, but when it comes to our children, that's another matter.

'They's gonna take our chavvies off us,' cried the mothers. 'What is we to do, my Aunt?' they asked the old gal, 'What is we to do?'

Tearing at their hair, they looked to the older ones for advice, fearing to lose their beloved chavvies. I can still see the big teardrops running down faces screwed up in fear.

'They can do what they like to me,' said me Mam, 'but not me chavvies.'

'Where's our men at?' one young mother cuddling a baby cried. 'I wants me man here.'

'We all do,' said another. 'Put the kettle on and make yourself useful,' the young woman was told, not unkindly.

'What if they come back to take our chavvies?'

'In that case fetch yourselves a stout stick each – and get the kettles on the boil. They won't like the taste of boiling water in their faces.'

Outsiders could not imagine the fear these parents felt at the threat of losing their children. Their children were their very lives and I can quite believe that they would have killed to protect them, if it came to a fight. So the little common prepared for war. Some mothers wanted all we chavvies to be hid in the wood, some mothers hid theirs under the bed up in the wagons. Walking up and down like soldiers, armed with sticks and kettle-irons, the women guarded the chavvies.

Then, one by one, the men began to come back from work. They returned to madness, at first not believing what they were being told. Some threw their shirts off ready to take on whoever set foot on the common.

'They'll send in the army to take our chavvies,' one old man shouted, 'just like they did in the War. They took my dear Theodore and I never seen him no more – and he only a child of sixteen. It killed me woman, that did, it took my poor Elsie what with the worry and pining. She died of a broken heart, that she did.'

All agreed to this, for poor Elsie had indeed died crying for her only son.

'Let's pack up, my Len, and make a run for it. If we all splits up and hides round the lanes, they won't find us.'

'No, we'll stay put tonight. There's enough of us to put up a fight. Let's ask the rest of 'em and work out what's best to be done.'

Shut up in the wagons, it was difficult to hear what was being said. But no grown-up slept that long night. They had their ears cocked, listening for the sound of lorries or anything with an engine coming close to the common. All through the night we heard, 'Hark, hark', when one or t'other of them thought they heard something.

There were so many questions asked by one and all and so much unrest: 'Any road, who is these people that they can tell us to stop travelling and give up the only life we know to stop on some camp?', 'How would we get our living if we was forced off the roads?'

Come morning, we chavvies was brought out to be washed and fed, then put back in the wagons. All the families pulled off the common, each fearful that at any minute they would lose their chavvies. Many sleepless nights and worried days followed. Each time we pulled in, we chavvies could not play but was made to keep our yocks peeled for police or cars – if we heard a car in the distance we had to run and hide.

Each time we shifted we was hidden, each time we pulled in we was hidden and the families kept a yock out for any gavver mushes who they thought could take their chavvies from them. This time in our lives must have been similar to that of families many generations ago, when they had to run and hide. The only difference was there were very few places left to hide – our stopping places and farm work were well known to the law so a lot of families like ours would hide their children in the wagons under the bunk bed. This was to be our way of life for months to come.

I was no longer allowed to help me Mam knock the doors.

'This is a dog's life. Why should we have to live like this? Why should we have to hide?' me Dad said one morning as me Mam got ready to walk off hawking her pegs. 'It's enough to make a man commit murder.'

'Don't talk like that in front the chavvies, you'll fret 'em unto death,' cried me Mam. 'Please, my Len, dick after me chavvies while I'm gone.'

'I'll guard 'em with me life,' he told her.

Gradually, as we moved around, we began to meet other Travellers and heard tales of children being taken from families in other parts of the country. From what we heard, there was nigh on murder done to those that took the children but the little ones were never found. Those we met over the years who had lost children were still grieving.

'If my little Jimmy had been killed, I would have a grave to sit by,' one poor mother said, 'but living like this, not knowing, is worse than death. It's a living death I got now. I don't know if me chavvy is alive or dead – I can't bear it,' she cried.

It took some time for the news to filter through that a lot of families had had children taken off them: very young children, toddlers and four- and five-year-olds – older children were more often left with their families.

In due course camps were built (which I have written about in my first book, *Our Forgotten Years*), camps built on old refuse tips, bogs, even cemented-over cemeteries, anywhere that was unsuitable for dwelling houses to be built on.

These are things that stuck in my and Alfie's minds over the years, because our parents' fear took all the magic from our young lives and left a bad memory. At first I couldn't write about this episode that has haunted me – I had no proof it ever really happened, only the memory of being hunted and hidden, of we Romanies' fear for our children. But it never left me and I never forgot what happened – the authorities could cover up what they had done, but they couldn't erase the memory of it in my mind or in the memories of the parents that lost these children.

It was not until I became an activist for my people in my later years and was invited to join various groups that I began to talk about what had happened when I was young. Yes, I would be told, we've heard of that, which gave me hope of finding out what did happen to our children that were taken from their families and never heard of again. They seemed to have vanished into thin air. Then one day I was at a meeting in the chambers of Lord Avebury, who campaigns for Gypsy rights, in the House of Lords. I'd been to this regular meeting a few times before and it was usually the same people who attended, but on this day there were two strangers.

At the House of Lords after a meeting with Lord Avebury.

They were two Romani Gypsies that had heard of our group and had come to ask our help in tracing their brothers and sisters who had been taken from their families back in the Fifties. I felt both elated and very sad at the same time, for here was two strangers talking about the dark deeds that had haunted me for years: it was out in the open at last. Here stood two people asking the very same questions as I myself had been asking for many a year. At last I felt free to speak and so I told my tale in public for the first time – the horror of that day when the government men visited the families on Chapel Plaister common. I felt I had been proved right and that all the sweeping under the carpet would stop now. Because sometimes I thought I must have dreamed it as no one was willing to believe me. Alas, we could not help the two strangers, we had no information to offer them, but at least I was not the only one asking why our children were still missing.

What were called 'camps' became known as 'sites' – those built in the Fifties that brought fear and sorrow to so many families still exist today, dotted all over the country, even though the first people that were forced onto them are no longer with us. Those were the people who were told to give up their nomadic lifestyle and settle down in one place or else their children would be taken away and put into care to be educated. That was history repeating itself: how many times going back through the centuries has my race been ordered to give up their nomadic life? You only have to read our history to know how many times that has happened.

Finally, in 2010 I believe it was, thanks to the Freedom of Information Act, word came from Canada: your children were sent out to us after the Second World War and some of them were horribly badly treated. I cried as I read the reports – I read and read, looking for the word 'Gypsy', but it was not there. All I found was references to 'underprivileged children', sent abroad. Well, maybe some of the poor little gorgie children that was sent out at the same time as our children were underprivileged, but my lot certainly were not underprivileged in any way. We never was starving or wet and cold – no Gypsy child went to bed hungry. Our parents were too good at providing for us to let us go hungry. We had good clean beds to sleep in and a wagon kept warm by the queenie stove in winter.

And as for our children so cruelly ripped from their families' embrace and sent overseas, we shall never know. Did they lose their identity? I like to think not, for the blood that runs in our veins is thick, kushti Gypsy blood. I wonder how they fared in a strange land and no one speaking their language? It would be good if, after all these years, the government would now admit that they took our children and for no good reason shipped them out the country, just because we are a nomadic race. To my mind, it was an attempt to eradicate our young generation.

As for the idea of providing sites, that too fell by the wayside, for they didn't build enough to accommodate our growing population. At the same time, they continued to find new ways of stopping us from travelling and leading our traditional lifestyle.

It's hard for the gorgie population to understand what we have gone through for hundreds of years. The reason I named this book *After All These Years* is because I am so very proud of my race and the fact that we are still here after all the things that have been heaped on our heads – treatment that would have destroyed a weaker race. No, good people of this England, we are going nowhere. This land is our home.

We cannot turn back the clock, but we can keep our colourful history alive, we can be proud to be related to our forefathers. And we can remember the Holocaust victims. We were all born Gypsies under the sun, rain, snow, wind and hail – with skin of a darker shade and eyes that flash in happiness and sorrow. I am lucky in that, unlike Gypsies in the past, I can and do speak up for my race. Day after day I shout, 'Yes, I am a Romani Gypsy – and very proud to be one.' The tide has turned – because there are others like me out there working to help keep our traditions and culture alive. I'm now seventy years old and my pride and passion at being a Romani Gypsy have not dimmed. I feel proud when I am able to help my race.

Since I started this book, I've felt it's time to call a truce on both sides. People are not all the same, and there's good and bad in all walks of life, but now there's just a chance we could all trust each other for the first time in hundreds of years.

There's been so much good work carried out by various Gypsy and Traveller groups, people who have dedicated their lives to bringing about a better understanding of us Gypsies and to argue the case for our needs in the areas of accommodation, healthcare, education, to name just three.

Many people have given up so much of their own lives, travelling all over the country to attend meetings. For a while I felt we were making progress for a better relationship between ourselves and the settled community. We needed to educate and break down barriers that had

Gypsy elder talks to housing group about their culture

A SOMERSET gypsy elder has been educating housing association staff about the ways of her culture.

Maggie Smith-Bendell spoke to workers at Yarlington Housing Group – which supplies affordable homes across South Somerset – after her recent successful visit to Wadham School in Crewkerne.

About 35 travellers met with pupils in July and set up an authentic camp to give an insight into their culture's history.

Meeting community safety officers at the Yeovil-based housing association following Gypsy Roma Traveller History Month, Mrs Smith-Bendell explained some of the problems currently faced by Romanies as common land is fenced off and stopping places are removed.

She also highlighted the importance of having a recognised address to allow children to have access to health care and education, and outlined difficulties faced by her people from the prejudices of others, often resulting in them hiding their identity to enable them to get the services they need.

She said these issues had driven many Romany gypsies to seek social housing even though it conflicted with many aspects of their culture.

Mrs Smith-Bendell, who is also chairman of the UK Association of Gypsy Women, said: "Many of my community live in south Somerset and have long and established family links in the area.

"My work involves a considerable amount of engagement with agencies like Somerset Racial Equality Council.

"It is vital for community relations for more events like Gypsy Roma Traveller History Month to be delivered so that the community can learn more about the Romany gypsy travellers.

"We are, after all, the oldest minority ethnic group in Somerset."

KNOWLEDGE SHARED: Maggie Smith-Bendell meets with Susan Savage from the Somerset Racial Equality Council and Yarlington Housing Group community safety officers Rachel Napper and Liam Canham.

Meeting with some of Somerset's housing and equality worker, Western Gazette.

been in place for hundreds of years, but I was beginning to see a dim light at the end of the tunnel – a light that would grow brighter with more work and increasing understanding. But, alas, my dream was shattered with the coming of the new Coalition government which has made it clear that Gypsies and Travellers seeking planning permission for private sites will get rough justice. For us Romanies history is repeating itself once again: gone is the chance to heal old wounds and convince people that we need somewhere to live, that we are willing to pay for a base from which to live our traditional lifestyle insofar as we still can. Here is hatred rearing its ugly fat head once again against a race of people in dire need. So we are back to square one and the fight will continue to simmer for years to come.

When will the government wake up and realise the size of the problem? There are now three groups fighting for space: a huge number of Irish Travellers, an ever-growing number of New Travellers also seeking somewhere to live, and then there's us, the Romanies of this country, whose numbers are also growing by the year.

It has got harder and harder for all these groups to find somewhere to live. A big reason for this, over the years, has been the increasing mechanisation of farm work – the loss of this work and the stopping places that went with it have dealt a huge blow to my community. Add to that the fact that so much of the common land has been fenced off and the police given more powers to move us on. Life became a game of chess: move one step at a time, dodge the law, avoid being evicted if you can.

All three groups have a recognised need not only to get off the highways but to gain access to services such as healthcare and education. The problem won't go away, so now is the time to work with our activist groups to start sorting it out.

Our ways are not your ways, our lifestyle is not yours. You have your heritage and we have ours. Had it not been for people over the centuries teaching you to look upon us with suspicion and distrust, I doubt you would give us a second glance – we would be just a part of English life, accepted for who we are. We are more than willing to help ourselves and take the burden off the taxpayer. But we need somewhere to live, just like anyone else. Let my race prove for once and for all – after all these years – that we are willing to compromise and work with others, to make a better world for all of us to live in. It's time to live in peace.

Chapter Seven

Looking Back

GOING BACK NOW to the nineteenth century, we Gypsies had more freedom than we had had in past centuries. Some of those terrible old laws had been repealed – although a new Turnpike Law had been introduced in 1822 which meant that any Gypsies found camping on the side of main roads could be heavily fined. This did make a difference to their travelling pattern – and cost them a great deal in fines. As a result they began to seek out the old green lanes away from the turnpikes and to make more use of the common lands – woods, spinneys and copses.

Their stopping places were well established by now, though. Families had their areas to which they would return to see out the harsh winter months. They knew where the springs and clean brooks were and they had them mapped out in their minds, in relation to the stopping places. Land and farm work would earn them their living in season. They also made pegs and wooden flowers along with their age-old potions and medicines. They were self-sufficient. Their skills came in handy – they had learned the art of hedge-laying and stone-walling, for instance. They began to bury their loved ones in local cemeteries, for we know of headstones going back to this time. And they was free to speak their own Romani language without fear of being brought to book and shipped out the country.

Among these people would have been me great Grandad (on me Dad's side) and his Dad. Even back then they would have been based in and around Somerset and Wiltshire. And at the same time somewhere in Devonshire would have been me Mam's family, the Smalls. I'm pretty sure of the name of Small, but not of me Dad's family name of Butler – because our Grandad, old Dannal Butler, once said one of his Grandads was from the Irish community.

I know the name of Smith came from the old Granny, who I don't think ever did marry up with me Grandad – so there was two surnames in me family: Butler and Smith. Me Dad took Smith as did his brothers Tom and Jim, Dan and Jessie. But their brother Joe took Butler which was his father's name – and their brother Alfie thought he wanted neither and chose his own name of Loveridge, quite why no one knew. Then their other brother John thought he liked the name of Symes, so gave himself that. As for me Dad's two sisters, Emily and Jane, they took their mother's name of Smith, until they married. I don't think any of me Dad's brothers or sisters were registered at birth. In the era in which they were born (were he alive today me Dad would be well over 90 years old), the family was constantly moved on and hence there are very few birth certificates in me Dad's family. Their lack of education didn't help matters either. It wasn't the same in me Mam's family for Grandad Jim Small stayed put around Plymouth and Newton Abbot in Devonshire and me Mam's birth was registered in Plymouth. Grandad Small never travelled far from his home area, unlike me Dad's family, who never stopped travelling long distances which took them to Dorset, Wiltshire, Herefordshire and Oxfordshire, their home base being Somerset and Wiltshire.

Without a birth certificate, when our men and women grew old they couldn't obtain pensions. I well remember trying to get one for me Dad.

It took nearly two years of letters going back and forth. In the end me Mam got so frustrated with the Pensions people, she had me write to them that me Dad was hatched out of a snake's egg. Thinking that would be the end of that, it was surprises all round when a pension book arrived – only for me Dad to throw a fit about not wanting charity! The book was duly sent back, so it was all for nothing. All of which was not too big a surprise because Gypsies would never accept charity. They had to provide for their own: to do otherwise would be a loss of face. Hence me Dad going without.

This Turnpike Law was still in force when I was a child and travelling with me family on the roads. It was not repealed until 1981. It was the reason for many an up and down with the Law or the old gavver mush. Having stopped for the night after travelling most of the day, our grys needing rest, food and water and ourselves in need of the same, a yog would be lit to cook on and boil the kettle. If we were lucky, no officer would appear, but if one did and he asked or ordered us to put out the yog, he might well kick it out himself. And he would not be too particular about kicking it over us chavvies as we sat round it. And some of the time he'd take five shillings off me Mam for lighting the yog – that was a heavy fine back then. Once it was paid, me Dad would throw his shirt off and offer to fist-fight the gavver to win the fine back (which was never accepted as far as I can remember). So, yes, I well remember the Turnpike Law.

When we caught up with other families it would be time to sit and tell the old tales again – terrible stories of the gavvers kicking out yogs, little chavvies who had had burning embers kicked in their faces and been scarred or disfigured for life, fathers who had then beaten up the culprit, only to land in jail, doing time for protecting their family.

Around the fire the old timers would relate tales from their grandads' times, going back well into the 1800s. Hence little scraps of actual happenings got passed down to us, but sounding so unbelievable that it did not seem as though it could be real. The people in charge would not do such things – how wrong we were not to believe our old folks' tales and to let this knowledge die out along with the tellers.

I well remember hearing me dear old Grandad Dannal repeat things *his* Dad and Grandad had told him, and they got dismissed with the shake of a head as being far-fetched. What an injustice was done to him, because now I know his tales were true. Tales of his uncle being hanged for crimes he was nowhere near, just because he was pointed out as being a Gypsy or relatives being deported for begging. Yes, to me Dad's generation it did sound far-fetched, but on reading our history I well believe me Grandad was telling the truth. I now see me Grandad in a new light. I understand the love he showered on his family, and I understand the rules he lived by: never trust a gorgie; never trust a gavver; never let 'em hear or learn 'em our language. Those are just a few of his strict rules, which he kept to his dying day.

How would this dear old mush feel today if he knew what I was doing with me life?: working on police diversity, talking and working with government officials – he would not only turn in his grave but start spinning. I can hear him now saying, 'You bad wench, Maggie.' Oh no, he would not understand – and why should he and the rest of his generation, whose families were treated worse than animals? Grandad, we of this generation cannot let our people be abused as your generation was back then, because you had no one to speak up for you. That's no surprise, you had to keep your heads down and hide away, not speak unless spoken to. It's different now, Grandad – we are not afraid any more. God bless your soul, old Dannal Butler, me dear Grandad, your granddaughter and many like her is here shouting out loud and clear: 'We are Romani Gypsies and proud of it. Do your worst – we will fight back to keep our race intact.'

I feel I owe no apology to past generations of my people for what I now do. I need to help, in my small way, to keep the Gypsy race going for the next few hundred years. So come on out, all my Gypsies out there, we are worth far more than the way we and our ancestors have been treated for hundreds of years. Our race is unique; let's all work together to keep it that way. Let's pull together as we once did and make full use of our culture and skills. Let's prove ourselves worthy of the old Gypsies in this chapter, those who brought us to this country, they who lost their lives for being Gypsies and different to others. We have *our* freedom at great cost to our ancestors. Remember what they went through and be proud of what you are.

It made no matter how we lived our lives, the Law was always just a step in front of us or behind us to harass us and move us on from their area. This was one of the reasons land work was important – we could pull off the road on to farmland. I saw so many things that made an impression on me: our womenfolk being given verbal grief when out hawking; the police tormenting our menfolk with a gleam of enjoyment in their eye; a woman going up into a wagon and staying there for days on end before reappearing with a new infant in her arms; me Dad's mares disappearing and coming back a few days later with a foal at foot; the magic of elder sticks being whittled into beautiful flowers – oh so very many Gypsy ways that make up the memories of a bygone lifestyle, of a group of people happy in their own way but struggling to exist, still believing that their way was the only way of life for them. After hundreds of years of harassment and prejudice, we were lucky to even have a life.

All in all it doesn't take much to make these families happy – just a bit of leeway and understanding of their needs. In my memory, I'm walking beside me Mam down a village street, smelling of carbolic soap as we knock on doors trying to persuade the housewives to buy a bunch of flowers or a dozen clothes pegs. Or I'm just leaning on me Dad's hip as we sit round the yog, listening to the old tales. Or going up in our wagon to get to bed in sweet-smelling blankets and a whiff of polish hanging in the air.

Chapter Eight

Life on the Road

IN ME GRANDAD'S TIME, life was all about walking. If our lot travelled ten miles in a day, those ten miles was walked. If a family was rich enough to hang on to the horses they bred, then they would be able to rig up some sort of transport (once the animals had come of age), but having such a big old family to keep and feed, *our* horses was sold off at fairs or to farmers, to make ends meet.

In his younger years me Grandad would earn extra vonger at fist-fighting. Although this was a sport among the Romani men, if one got a reputation for being able to use his fists, it could and often did lead to a challenge for vonger – which was right up Grandad Dannal's street. He would fight other Romani men as well as gorgies – anyone who would give it a go. These fights were clean and fair – winner takes all.

Me Dad and his brother Jessie were two ringtails and loved nothing better than a kushti old punch-up. 'Ringtail' is a Romani word for a person who is always up to mischief and willing to fight at the drop of a hat – and me Dad and his brother were proper ringtails. They were not so organised as Grandad, who would study his challenger and note his best points or moves. No, not these two – they would throw down a challenge and fight on the spot. Win or lose, they were in their element.

I remember, too, me Dad getting up and jumping out the wagon like a spring chicken at four o'clock in the morning, ready to fight another Travelling man – a fist-fight of honour, it was said – both enjoying the challenge and giving best to each other at the end. Giving best is when a man meets his match in a fight – a man just as good as he is with his fists so that they could fight for hours with no real winner coming out of it – they will agree to give best to each other and end the fight. Both will go their separate ways with bloody noses and split lips, maybe minus a few teeth where they've caught an unlucky blow.

But as young chavvies Dad and Jessie had it rough, which made them grow up into hard men, as all Romani chavvies did back then. Compared to their young years, ours were a piece of cake with sugar on it. *We* never had to sutty (sleep) under the wagon. The only time *we* chavvies walked when shifting on to other stopping places was when we cried to be let out of the confines of the wagon, to run along behind our wagon and horses on quiet country roads or lanes. That was fun for us but a worry to me Mam and Dad who couldn't see what we was up to, walking and playing out of sight behind the wagon. To judge from the old stories, Grandad's generation was even worse off: working in the fields all day and sleeping on the ground under a canvas sheet at night. The winters – and they really were winters – made them old afore they were grown.

I can never remember me Grandad as anything other than old and bent, with swollen hands and legs. They said it was the gout. His skin was like polished leather, drawn tight over his swollen head. But he was the nicest of all Grandads. His old heart was golden, he loved and cared for us all – no matter who our mother might be.

Unlike me old Granny, who hated the sight of us because she'd got it into her old scraggy head that me Mam was a gorgie. No amount of proof could change her mind, not even when she met me Mam's people on the pea fields. Gran could work in those fields alongside one of the oldest Romani families from Devonshire and still call me Mam 'That old gorgie wench'. Me Dad would laugh and tell me Mam, 'My Vie, you can't educate pork,' but I think she was downright jealous of me Mam, for she was young and as pretty as paint and could hold her own amongst any of me Dad's family when it came to hawking and field work.

Me Mam never really lost her looks. When she died, aged eighty-five, she was still a pretty woman and would dress her tiny body in smart clothes. Her hair had to be just right even after all her years. When she was happy her smile would light up the place, unlike me old Granny who had a permanent sneer on her chops and never knew how to smile.

But give the old woman her due. She was brought up in a big family in very hard times and when it came to feeding her family one or two shussies (rabbits) would go nowhere: she would cook six or seven in the big black pot, topped up with taters, swede and carrots. (When Gypsies with big hungry families shifted on, pheasants and shussies was often scarce on the ground where they had been!) Oh yes, even if she couldn't smile, she knew how to cook (her suet puddings were much talked about).

Me Grandad had saved up for many a day to buy his first wagon – either a Burton or a Reading. He finally found one he could barely afford up in the hop country. He chopped (that is, he agreed to swop) everything he owned worth anything to get it. It was a big, wooden high-wheeled wagon that made his yocks pop out when he saw it. After the hops had been picked the deal was done.

Grandad had his wagon, which had a little iron stove and chimney; his old faithful gry would pull it. Grandad and Emma (me Granny) had their first ever bed too. He was made up and proud of his deal.

As they all got ready to leave the hop country, the Traveller man he had had the wagon off come over and tried to sell Grandad another horse, telling him he would need one.

'What do I need another gry for?' he asked.

'Because with a wagon that size you needs a tracer.'

'Naw, I don't.'

'Yes you do. Your old gry won't pull that wagon up the steep hills – or hold it back going down the hills, my son.' (Most men would keep a second horse, known as a tracer, to hitch to the sharve [shaft] to help pull a heavy wagon up a steep hill.)

'I'm a telling you,' said Grandad, 'I don't need me no tracer, even if I could afford one.'

'Like me dead father, you do,' said the Traveller.

'I got me six kushti tracers,' answered Grandad.

'Where's that at then?' asked the Traveller.

'Stood there, look.' And he pointed to his sons. 'They's me tracers, up hill and down. I'll put a halter round their waists and make use of 'em – tie 'em to the sharves if I have to, the useless objects. It's time they earnt their keep...'

According to me Dad, Grandad got the wagon back safe and sound to Wiltshire, using his sons as grys. Once there, he put them all to work to earn another gry that could be used for breeding and as a tracer.

It was in this same wagon that, not many months later, me old Granny rolled over in the night and squashed little Iky, her young baby, and he was buried up in Wiltshire in a bloater box. So her first bed brought her no luck. Losing infants in this way was not uncommon back then.

Yes, me old Grandad was a bright spark in his younger days, but he had his hands full with his sons. When me Mam and Dad got together and had us, we still travelled to visit Grandad in his old stopping places where he'd tell us tales of long-ago happenings. Some were sad such as poor Iky's end and some were very funny, such as the one about the day he was washing his horse in a river and along came a lady riding a bike. She stopped and screamed at him, accusing Grandad of trying to drown his horse.

'What be you on about, woman?'

'You wicked, wicked man, drowning that poor horse!'

'Drowning me hoss? Missus, this hoss is worth more than you is.'

'I'm getting the law on you,' she shouted and pedalled off as if her life depended on it before he got a chance to explain that the hoss needed a wash and thoroughly enjoyed having one. So he just carried on shaking his old head and thinking that some folks were crackers, off their heads.

'I washed me gry,' he'd go on, 'and had walked it back to me wagon. I was giving it a good rubbing down with a handful of dried grass while Emma made a brew of tea – me and me gry both happy as sandlarks. Then Emma tells me, "Oh doughty, Dannal, here comes the gavver and a woman." I'd been expecting it, so I say, "Stay put and you'll bust yer gut a-laughing when yis hears what that woman accused me of."

Now the woman is pointing at me – "That's him, that's the man that drowned the poor horse!" The gavver, knowing me because this was one of our regular stopping places, said, "Dannal, have you drowned your horse?"'

'Well, if I did, this one here must be its bloody ghost.'

The gavver had to smile. 'Dannal, did you try to drown your horse?'

'Yis knows full well when I stops here I sometimes washes me hoss in the river. And it's so shallow I'd have a job on me hands to drown that old daft woman who's brought yis here. Drown the only thing I own that's worth its weight in gold – that woman's barmy, she should be locked up.'

'Are you satisfied no crime has been committed?' the gavver asked the old woman.

'I don't trust these people,' she answered.

'And by God, Missus, we don't trust dinalows like you,' said Emma. 'Now hit the road and don't come back. You mind your business and we'll mind ours.'

'Off went the woman. We watched till she was well up the road, then all three of us burst out laughing,' Grandad told us.

'That was a waste of your time,' he told the gavver.

'Not at all, Dannal. Knowing how you people values your horses, I just had to see your face when I turned up with your accuser.'

'Yeah,' said Grandad, 'I had half a mind to hide me hoss in the farmer's field and have that woman running up and down the river bank, searching for a drowned hoss, but I thought better of it.'

'So, will you be moving on in the next day or two, Dannal?' asked the gavver mush.

'Yeah, me an' Emma will hit the road on the morrow – and yis kin earn a pint in the pub with the tale of the drowned hoss.'

'I just might do that, Dannal. See you next time you're around this way.'

We loved to hear me Grandad's tales. He was once accused of cruelty for putting sack bags on his gry's feet when travelling on a freshly tarmacked road. The bags were used to stop the tarmac getting packed hard into its hooves, because the tar would burn its feet and make the gry lame, not to mention giving it pain. But one house dweller thought it would hurt the gry and kicked up a merry old fuss, crying 'Shame on you, treating a dumb animal in this way.'

'If you don't mind your own business, Missus, I'll tie bags on *your* feet. Now hop it.'

And many a time passers-by would see freshly caught rabbits hung up and accuse the Traveller families of cruelty.

'Ain't yis ever had rabbit stew?' they would be asked. 'Of course yis have. Now we're having ours.'

Yes, you never knew what you would be accused of while travelling the roads. We seemed to draw people's comments and accusations like iron to a magnet.

Me Mam would take me out calling with her, me Dad having duly warned me not to take anything that wasn't mine. In late spring and all summer long, I really enjoyed hawking with me Mam, but the winters was colder and I wanted to stay put by our yog.

'Come on, my Maggie, and give your Mam a hand today, there's a kushti gal. I'll beg yis something kushti, that I will,' she'd tell me.

Grandad liked to travel round Somerset, it was his favourite area. There were so many scattered little villages that we could spend months, if need be, hawking between Cheddar, Wells and Midsomer Norton, travelling a few short miles every couple of days. The old Granny would take off in one direction and us two in the other. So for instance if we were pulled in near Blagdon, say, close to the lake, Mam and I would set off to call up the lanes towards Langford while the old woman would go down to Ubley and Compton Martin.

We knew some kind people in most of these outlying places: farmers who would chop (barter) a lump of cheese, butter or a few eggs for pegs or flowers. And if our luck held a pot of jam could be had. Apples we helped ourselves to – most every road we took we passed an orchard full of apples or plums. Blackberries was picked both to sell and to be cooked in blackberry and apple dumplings. Finding food or clean water were not our biggest problems. We could survive where house-dwelling people would starve: we had been taught how to by experts of our race.

I enjoyed calling the doors – especially if they had not been called by others for a few months. We had more than one lady house-dweller that would save her children's clothes for us. Over the years they had got to learn our travelling habits and were not too surprised when we knocked their doors.

These days I quite often get invited to speak to older people in rest homes and village halls. It may surprise you that even now, in 2012, I make bunches of wax roses and wooden chrysanthemums as well as clothes pegs to take along to remind them of when they were young – the things we sold to their mothers and grans. I always get a good welcome and we all travels back in time together.

I recently got an invite to the little village of Bradpole near Bridport in Dorset. I took along my hawking basket filled with traditional flowers. I was booked to talk from 7.30 to 8.30pm and I was still trying to get away at 9.45 pm. We all had a grand night: the ladies enjoyed bringing back the memories that they'd thought were long forgotten and they gave me many names of the travelling families they remembered stopping in their area.

I was asked so many questions about our life as it is today compared to back then and the amount of interest they showed pleased me so much, not to mention the nice genuine comments they made about when we were all young. And my hawking basket was good and empty when I left. I gave them the flowers to share among themselves, which brought smiles all round.

A good sixty years and more passed between the time when I used to go out hawking the doors with me Mam and when I started to be invited to give talks about the old days.

But to go back now to when I was a little gal, running like a deer up and down front paths and steps to knock on dwelling house doors where we hoped to sell our wares...

Me Mam would keep a yock on me as we both hawked. 'Don't go too far ahead of me, my Maggie, and stay in earshot.' Sometimes a lady would want more of what I had in me hand and I would call to me Mam for more, or me Mam would want me to take the side of the street that had longer garden paths because I could skip up them quicker than her.

We called many kinds of dwellings, some very posh and some very poor-looking. It was not their possessions I noticed as much as the toys their chavvies had. I would gaze at the dolls' pram left out in the rain. Oh, I would look after it better than that, I used to think. The lovely dolly thrown in a corner – how I would treasure that doll if she was mine. But toys were not for us. We had no room to carry such useless things in our wagon. But one day, I promised meself, I too would have dollies and prams – and most of all a dolls' house of me very own (which in my old age I do now have).

When out hawking, if I was given a pot of homemade jam or honey, I would brag that I had got it to share with the family.

'Is yis enjoying yer bread an' jam, our Alfie? I begged yis that.'

'No yis never did, me Mam begged it.'

'You never, did yis, Mam? I got it, didn't I just?'

'Yes, yis did, my Maggie. Shut up, Alfie, and leave her be.'

I must brag a little more. Me and me Mam hawking on our own always did very well for ourselves, with no competition from other Travellers knocking the doors. We could take our time and hawk ourselves out and look forward to the next day's calling too.

We travelled for a few months with our grandparents and then we came across others of me Dad's family who changed places with us. That meant we were travelling on our own once again. This made me Mam very happy. She loved it being just her little brood and being able to please ourselves which road to take. But for days we chavvies would miss our old Grandad and wish he was still travelling with us – but not so the old Granny.

We travelled on to Binegar, a little tiny hamlet above Shepton Mallet, where we found me Dad's brother John and his woman Ellen pulled in with their young family. While the two women went out hawking, me Dad and Uncle John made them clothes pegs to sell. We stayed in Binegar Lane for a few weeks, then split up and once again found ourselves on our own. It was time to decide which way to head.

'Bristol,' me Dad said. 'My Vie, I'll take you to a common I've not took yis to before. We can have ourselves a kushti stop there.'

'Whereabouts is it?' asked me Mam.

'Right on the other side. You'll think it a kushti place.'

Aunt Ellen and Roy selling flowers in Sidmouth.

And so we took the road that brought us out at Green Ore, then on through Farrington Gurney. We turned off for High Littleton, then on through Marksbury towards Keynsham. We stopped for the night before we got to Keynsham to give our grys a break.

On the morrow we reached Siston Common.

'It dicks a kushti place, my Len,' laughed me Mam, 'but we can't stop here. Just you dick at all the tents and wagons. There's too many other Travellers here, we shan't earn our bit of living amongst this lot.'

'You'm dead right, my Vie, I made a big bloomer, but we must pull up and pass the time of day with some of 'em.'

It was mostly the Ayres families – Bristol was their base ground and most of 'em was stopping right here. Although they would travel up to the hop country and down around the pea country, this was their main area where they would return at the end of the season, much the same way as we returned to Wiltshire and Somerset. This common was one of the most popular ones to stop on because of the big town and surrounding built-up areas. We knew full well that the dwellings within walking distance would have been hawked to death by the many mothers and young gals already on the common (and by the look of things there was over twenty families already here looking for the very same thing as ourselves). Because there were so many families already scattered over the common, we would have had to catch buses to other parts of Bristol to hawk our pegs, if we had stayed there. This way of hawking was hard work and the bus conductor would always grumble about having the big hawking baskets on the bus because they took up too much room.

So, having passed the time of day with the other families and thanked them for the offer to pull in, on we travelled.

'This road will lead us over to the Novers, where our boy Robert was born,' said me Dad. 'It'll take us the best part of the day, but we'll get there.'

'That was a kushti common,' remarked me Mam, 'but it was no kushti to us my Len.'

'Never mind, my Vie, the Novers is just as good. Plenty of tans [houses] for you and young Maggie to call.'

Although the Novers was a prime stopping place, no other wagons were around as we pulled off the road and made our camp. While me

Mam prepared our meal, me Dad went off pegsticking – cutting hazel sticks to make a few gross of pegs. On the morrow I would go out hawking with me Mam, both to give her some company and to keep me and that little mush our Alfie apart. Me Mam always liked to call in pairs, because all through her young life, afore she had me Dad, it was her and her sister Ellen who hawked together each day. She had got used to this way of calling, so with me by her side it felt like her old life. Had she not took me, there was nothing surer than that Alfie and me would have got to fighting each other. So to keep the peace we got split up. Although all through his short bit of life (he died in 1985 at the age of 47) he and I loved each other to death, we could never agree on anything much and would fight like two juckles. He bossed me about but he also protected me when the situation called for it – he was my hero on many occasions. And my worst enemy on others. But most of all he was me big brother and I loved him dearly. I miss him and his antics to this very day.

Alfie was a very special person in my life. He knew so much about wildlife and often would whisper, 'Come with me, I got something to show you.' It could be anything from a nest of birds to fish in the river.

Once while we were stopped on Maiden Down between Taunton and Tiverton he found a little white effet (lizard) laying in the sun. Maiden Down is known for these little harmless effets – there's thousands there – but this was an albino one and he shared his discovery with me.

'You've never dicked the like, have you, our Maggie?' he said quietly.

'No, our Alfie. The sun must have bleached it white.'

'You gert dinalow, this is a special one. It was born this colour. And don't tell the rest, they might mour [kill] it.'

Yes, it *was* a special one, because he felt he could only show it to me. Funny how things stick in one's mind over sixty or seventy years.

We two bonded when young and would stand back to back and fight the village chavvies and grown-ups as we got older, when the need arose. He was slow to temper, but when it did flare up he could do the

76

business. I never feared for him in a fight.

He was never a tall chap but shortish and stocky. And, my, he was kushti-looking. All the bits of gals had a yock for him, which made me jealous. I could have took their lips off.

'You likes they old gals, our Alfie,' I often told him.

'And you is a gert big dinalow,' he would laugh, brushing back his mop of hair, feeling not a little proud of himself.

He was my friend and mentor.

As we rambled round the narrow lanes of the Novers with our little Jess and Robert tagging along behind, we had the world at our feet. We climbed the trees, played in the spring and got as dirty as they come. All the while knowing that just back down the road was our Mam and Dad, all and everything we needed in life. For these two people above all others were our protectors and would worry their lives away over us chavvies. Often, if we had been gone from their sight too long, me Mam would send me Dad dicking for us, in case we was hurt or in trouble.

'Go fetch they chavvies, my Len, I wants to scrub them, head, face and ears.' She would say this to allay her own fears – and me Dad's – in case anything should have happened to us.

As I've already mentioned, accidents among our Travelling families were not rare. Many little chavvies were maimed or killed either by the yogs, the grys or from falling out of wagons or trees. We ourselves were not usually aware of any dangers when we were playing together out of sight of our parents, but screams soon had them heading our way, threatening to kill us if we had hurt ourselves: panic brought out all kinds of reactions but mostly it was threats, out of their love for us. A few years later when I fell out of Kizzie's wagon on me head and needed stitches, me Mam screamed louder than me, and poor old Dr Williams had his hands full with her. 'Hush,' he told her, 'You're frightening your child!' but that's how Gypsy mams is. They panic and scream, while the dads tremble in fright.

So when we were out playing, there would eventually be remarks like, 'Better head back to the wagon now, our Maggie, afore they two comes dicking for us.'

'Aw, our Alfie, we ain't bin 'ere long. It's kushti, let's wash our feet in the cow trough.'

'Our Maggie, dick down the tober [road] yonder. It's me Dad, and he ain't out picking nuts. He's got a stick in his hand.'

That would be enough for me and off we would run to him, full of woe: 'Oh Dad, we fell in the trough, it was a mishap...'

'Your Mam will give you lot a mishap. Get going and take yer punishment,' he would laugh.

Yes, the lives of chavvies growing up on the road could be free and full of fun and laughter. Working in the fields beside our parents had its moments too, as did going out daily hawking the doors. We were taught not to bother folks or pick up anything that was not ours to take. We were taught to fear the Law and would keep our yocks full on a gavver if one appeared at our wagon or stopping place. As far as we were concerned, they meant us harm. There was no trust on our part towards these men of the Law.

Stopping on the outskirts of the big town of Bristol gave us plenty of opportunity to earn our living in peace for a few weeks. But soon me Dad had got itchy feet for the open road and we was on the move again, back down towards Wells. We pulled on the lanes of Priddy, where we met up with Bob and Polly Frankham. These two were close friends of me Mam and Dad, so we hitched up with them to go pea-picking. Bob hailed from Hampshire and I believe he met Polly while in the pea country of Somerset – his family used to travel down there to pick the peas – but I'm not fully certain how they met each other. What I do know is that they was a very happy couple and enjoyed their lives. They had travelled with me Mam and Dad well afore we chavvies was born. Polly was a very good-looking young woman, about the same age as me Mam, and Bob was tall and one of the kindest Traveller men I had met. He had been pals with me Dad for many a year.

Bob and Polly had a deep love for children and showed it to us and others in many ways. While travelling with them, if any one of us chavvies hurt themselves and cried, these two dear people would find us titbits to make things better – with an added cuddle. Bob had made our travelling area his own and would spend most all his time in the West part of the country. But they would also travel back across country once in a while to see his side of the family. A nicer couple you couldn't wish to meet, as me Dad used to say.

It was decided that we would pull on the headlands of the pea fields. That way we were right on the job. We'd cut out early morning travelling and have our homes with us where we worked.

As we got close to Bridgwater the two men rode their grys on ahead to the farm to book for the field work. We had a couple of weeks before the peas would be ready – this would give us ample time to get things ready for the long hot summer's work. A feeling of excitement grew in all of us. If the weather played fair, we intended to work hard and long and earn a fair amount of vonger. Then we would be able to wait around for Bridgwater Fair at the end of the season. So with that treat in mind, when the day come to start picking, every one of our little family joined in with relish.

The field was sweet with the smell of the peas, row upon row growing fat in the bright sunlight. And there we all were in a long line across the field, Travellers who had come many miles to get this work: young, old and even some ill or infirm – all eager and willing to earn their livelihood.

Nets were handed out by the grower – he would bring more once he was sure of the amount the shops and the London market would order from him. This would be his way of thinking right through the season: we would only pick the orders he was sure of. But we always picked Sundays to Fridays, earning as we worked. The number of times we had weighed in a 20lb net of peas was tallied up at the end of each day. Big families could earn big money, little families like ours could also do well enough.

Stopping on the 'headlin', as we called it, had many advantages. Not only did we have no travelling to the fields, our grys were tethered on the sweet untrodden grass. And our little banty hens could run free, scratching among the rows of peas alongside the partridges and pheasants who lived and bred on the fields.

Evenings our men would take the juckles out catching shussies or net them instead. Rabbits and pheasants come free, and with the farmer growing fields of taters and cabbages, broad beans and peas, it made vegetables easier to get hold of too. So during these long working seasons life for the community was a lot less stressful.

All chavvies aged three or over would pick the peas. At the age of three we would pick a bucketful. After a back-breaking day all we chavvies had to do was amble back to our wagons, but after having done a full day's pea-picking the women would start work on cooking and washing – and after that start getting us cleaned up for bed. Only then could they relax and have fun round the yogs.

In a kushti season pea-picking could last from the middle of May till July or early August, depending on the growing weather and how many late peas had been planted. The work was very important to us. It meant we were not travelling or getting in trouble with the police for stopping on the highways or having to walk miles each day knocking on doors. So it was much appreciated to be able to stop and work with no worries about where to go on the morrow.

Another plus was that mothers expecting to be confined could get hold of the doctor or midwife – which meant more live babies and mothers. Within our Travelling community there have always been a high number of deaths at birth and to be able to stop in one place long enough to get access to midwives and doctors was a big bonus, especially with a young mother having her first. Anything could happen – and all too often it did.

We did have a kushti season, but all too soon the peas started to run out. The families heading up to Hereford and the hop country were beginning to pull out. They had a long journey ahead of them on narrow roads. Barring no accidents such as a lame gry or a broken wheel or sharve, they would make it in good time to settle down afore the hop season started in late September. As for us, we hung on to pick the last of the peas, squeezing in a few extra days' work. We had made our minds up to attend the Bridgwater Horse and Sheep Fair.

Chapter Nine

Bridgwater Fair

IT WAS NOW SEPTEMBER and nigh on Bridgwater Fair. When the last pea-nets had left the field for the shops and markets, it would be our time to spruce things up. We had to look our best for the coming fair. So afore we left our stopping place on the headlin, the wagons would be cleaned and polished inside and out, pretty blankets washed and dried and the little pairs of net curtains laundered and freshly hung on doors and windows.

Our best clothes were took out and given an airing. Me Mam always kept a few tidy clothes for herself and me Dad to wear at fairs – and also some of the nicer chavvies' clothes she had begged or bartered for would have been folded and put away for just such times as this. We had to look kushti to match our wagons and grys. The grys would be as fat as ticks, not having been working for a good while but lazing on plug chains and filling their bellies instead. They looked as fit as fiddles and had a shine on their coats to match any glass bottle.

Looking like new pins, wearing the frocks, coats and jackets me Mam had begged for us, and me with new ribbon tied on the ends of me long plaits, we travelled over to the fair field and pulled in, every one of us feeling the excitement: we chavvies for the candyfloss and rides; the women looking forward to finding something pretty to put on show in their wagons. As for the men, they had many things on their minds: chopping and dealing – and a few beers to wash the pea dirt from their throats, or so they would say.

On first sight things looked fairly drab: just the fair folks working fast and furious to set up their rides and sideshows, their lorries and trailers pulled close together. The little stalls of sweets and toffee apples were already up. While our grown-ups walked off up the town to shop and have a drink, we chavvies stood in groups watching the fairground take shape. We'd been warned time and again by our parents and the fair folk alike to keep back, out of the way of the machinery. Because accidents *do* happen and people can get hurt or maimed. Also, everyone had to concentrate on the job in hand – the lives of the public depended on the skill of the fairground men who put the fair together. Once in a while you'd hear the boss flare up at a worker: 'Keep your mind on the job,' they were told in no uncertain terms, with a few colourful words thrown in for good measure. For the head mush would walk round constantly, checking on the progress of the work.

We missed nothing of the activity going on during the setting up of the fair. Some of the local young men were able to get odd jobs of work off the showmen and each year these young men waited as eagerly as we did, they to earn and we to spend and enjoy. These were nice young men who we had got to know over the years and from whom we could beg a free ride in and out, so we were all friendly towards each other.

The evening afore this particular fair we was sitting round our yog (one of many round the edge of the fairground), listening to stories about fairs of old, where great breeding grys had been bought or chopped out for, wagons that had been exchanged for another, a set of brass-buckled harness that was still being used ('A real tough leather set – yis can't beat a kushti bit of old leather harness,' said one old timer, set in his ways).

Everyone was in a jolly mood, having had a kushti day in the town. They had all worked hard in the pea fields and needed to relax and let off steam, now that the season was over. This fair would be just the place to let go and enjoy the big day on the morrow.

Deals was done on this night: anything with a little profit in it would be bought off other Travellers who had already pulled in and sold on tomorrow to someone else. Romani Gypsies make most of their living from chopping and dealing. To be a good dealer you have to let your eyes be your guide. For instance, if another Gypsy or a mush from the settled community has got a horse or cart for sale, you stand and take a deep look at it. If it's a horse you more or less vet it to make sure it's sound in body and limb. You listen to its breathing, look right in its yocks. You can tell a lot by the colour of the whites of its yocks. If it's got lots of scabs on its knees, leave it alone: it means it falls to its knees while pulling a load, so it has a weakness; it could well be that its lungs are packing up. Such grys are known as 'wids'. You check its age by looking in its mouth and counting the shells or ridges on its teeth.

And then you ask for it to be shown on the move. It is then held on its halter and run up and down. Its leg movements are watched closely, and the way it holds its head. Gypsy men are well-known for having a keen eye and very little gets past them. When it comes to horses, they have been involved with and working with grys since they could walk and have had the best of teachers to give them that special knowledge, their fathers and grandads.

So when a deal is in the offing, you judge the animal and its worth and make your mind up what to pay and what profit can be made on it. It's always been like this and always will be. Our men still deal today as they did back down through the generations – it's culture and custom, knowledge and skill.

It was late when we were put to bed, hardly able to sleep in anticipation of what a grand day we would have come morning. Our faces smarted from the scrubbing me Mam had given us, on the promise of a pocket of pennies each if we went straight to sleep. But having spent hours watching the fairground take shape and listening to all the tales round the yog, it was hard to get off to sleep. Me and our Alfie talked in hushed voices of what tomorrow would bring as we lay side by side under me Mam and Dad's bunk. Well, we thought we were talking quietly till there came a knock on the side of the wagon and me Dad's voice telling us to git to sutty or no fair for us...

In me mind's yock, I can still see that next morning. When the three of us (Alfie, Little Jess and me) woke, the wagon was dark and quiet. It was the smell of the smoking yog and frying bacon that brought us from our sleep. It was very early and the sky was thinking about lighting up for the day ahead. So, to the sound of the showmen stirring around their stalls and rides, we three chavvies climbed out the wagon and ran to the yog. Handed a hot cup of tea and a thick bacon butty, we was all set.

From a distance we watched the stalls slowly being filled with all the magic things of the fair. We saw the goldfishes in their round bowls: we would have liked one for our own, but we weren't allowed. The coconut shy was set up. We smiled at each other as we watched the men push the nuts well down in the cups of sand on stalks so that they would be difficult to knock out with the little round wooden balls. Then there was the shooting range where pellet guns would be used to knock down a target. The stall with the little ducks floating round in shallow water with hooks on top of their heads – they had to be hooked out the water and a number painted on the bottom of each had to be matched to a number painted on a board to win. There was very few wins on this game, I can vouch for that, because I tried many times to win a doll for meself, but never managed it.

Then there was the gingersnap and sweet stall, of great interest to us three, as our yocks was on the black and white bullseyes, which we was very fond of, given the chance. There was a candy-striped tent full of daft mirrors – looking in some you were as fat as a louse, in others as long and thin as a pegstick. I couldn't stick this tent – the one I would have liked to get into was the freak show, where the bearded lady and the little people were, but the mush guarding it and taking the vonger was too quick for us to sneak past. Best of all was the candy-tuff and toffee apple stall. I loved the smell and taste of the hot melting sugar.

The boxing booth was the main attraction for our young fist-fighters, who liked to have a go, win or lose. The ghost train was a no-go area – me Dad would not let us on it. He said we would be up all night with nightmares, although we had other ideas about that, but he told us we could try it out when we got older. The wall of death, where men would ride motorbikes up the wall as it spun round fast, was out of bounds too. Alas, we were only allowed to stand and watch. Me Dad was frit to death we could get hurt or worse. But the biggest thrill was the lights and music from all the rides, so bright and loud.

When we had rides both our parents would be there keeping an eye out for us. But then it would be their turn to have their fun and they'd get settled in the kitcherma. The kitchermas opened from ten o'clock in the morning till two o'clock, then would not open again till seven at night before finally shutting at ten. While we sat outside watching and waiting for chucking-out time, a bit of sport was had that day. A crowd came out the pub and made a ring on the grass: two young up-and-coming fist-fighters was going to square up to each other. Amid cries of 'Get back out the way, you chavvies, or you'll get hurt,' we was pushed right back. There wasn't even a wall for us to stand on to see the fight. And we were only three among dozens of chavvies all waiting for their parents and who were all made to move out the way.

'You Maggie, an' our Jess, come with me,' whispered our Alfie. 'Come on quick,' he said, heading for a big old hay wagon that had been used to transport things to the fair. 'Climb up on this and we'll get the best view,' he told us – as the word flew round the ground: 'Fight, *fight...*' – and more and more people come running.

High up on our perch, we could see everything. Each fighter's family stood behind their boy. The Traveller mush who was to see fair play stood between them.

'Fight fair and no kicking or biting,' they was both warned. Stripped to the waist, young and fit, they glared at each other, one spitting on the ground. We knew one of the fighters, so when the fight kicked off we called his name out. The noise was bedlam, as each family shouted to their fighter and the crowd joined in. Soon the blood and snot was flying. We could hear each punch smack on flesh, up and down the field the ring of people moved as one as the fight hotted up.

It seemed to last an age, till one lad went out for the count – and the fist of the other was held high.

'Let's get down and tell me Dad what we seen,' I said to Alfie.

'Not yet, you dinalow, it's not over yet.'

Sure enough, one of the boys' fathers challenged the other father to fight. We watched as the ring was again brought to order. Both the older men shook hands, unlike their sons. Then they too threw off their shirts and jackets – having worked the fields all summer they was as brown as berries. Thickset and fresh, they were ready to fight.

'May the best man win,' said the fair-play mush, adding, 'and no biting or kicking. Fight fair. Now get to it.'

This was a fight and a half. From our perch (now invaded by others), we stood on tiptoe to watch this pair nearly mour each other. Black hair wet with sweat, they fought long and hard, each one losing their footing at times but not staying down, both determined to put up as kushti a fight as they could. Up and down they went till at last the ref stopped the fight and held both their arms up. We watched as they held each other upright then shook hands. Afterwards, it was said that these two had fought for nearly an hour – and would have carried on till one was laid out, if the fight had not been stopped.

'Hold tight to your seat,' said our Alfie. 'It dicks like the two women gotta fight.' In some families, if the men fought then their women would fight each other as well.

'Oh doughty, our Alfie, you're right, they's gonna have a go too.'

This was not an unusual occurrence. I once watched me own Mam fight this way, after me Dad had had a fight. The women could be the best of friends before their men got fighting, but watching their husbands being punched or knocked down got the blood running hot and fast in their veins. Hearing another woman shouting for her man to finish off your man brought out the fighting spirit in you and bad feelings would erupt between the two wives. Then both women would be more than willing to give each other a hiding and even better if it was in public.

The crowd got really noisy as the two women ripped off their top layer of clothes and fought in their shimmies. It never lasted very long, but fight they did, as kushti as two men, exchanging blow for blow and punch for punch. Our women don't waste time pulling hair and scratching, they trade punches toe-to-toe just like their menfolk. These fights are taken very seriously and are subject to the same fair-play rules as the men. I felt sorry for the smaller one, thinking she would surely get beaten, as I strained me neck to watch them fight. You couldn't hear yourself speak for the hollering and shouting, then, lo and behold, the little 'un drew back and stretched out the bigger woman with a right upper cut. Fight over.

All in all neither family had anything to be ashamed of. It was kushti clean sport. They walked off as friends, but they would be added to our yogside tales in the future. Fights between two well-known families would be recorded in our tales – they had earned their reputation fair and square.

The police had been alerted to the fight by the shouts of the onlookers and had come running to break it up, but as usual they'd just been told that fist-fighting is one of our sports – well, it's only a little white lie. When things had got back to normal and the police had been pacified, me Dad put us all on the huge swing boats. Then both of them took us round the fair. Me Dad managed to win us a coconut and treated us to toffee apples. Then he disappeared in the boxing booth to watch some of our young men box. The women made their way back to the wagons to cook a bit of grub and feed whoever happened to be round the yog at the time.

Bridgwater Fair was only half over – we still had the rest of the afternoon and evening to go. When the pubs opened again the drinking and dealing would start. The sheep pens were half empty by now – the farmers were busy loading up what they had bought and heading home to catch up on the farm work, no time to laze about watching the antics of the Gypsy folk. Bridgwater Fair was a well-known sheep and horse fair so there were always lots of pens full of sheep and young lambs to be sold by an auctioneer. This part of the fair held little interest for us. It was the farmers' day for selling off unwanted stock, but once the auction was over the farmers would leave.

Now the grys was pulled out to be run up and down the fair field to prove how sound in wind and limb they were. And just you dick at me Dad, swinging on his mare's tail to show how quiet she is. If we attempted to do that, he would mour us. It was a mare he'd bought some time back and he knew her well – but all the same, she might kick back and knock his brains out.

Me Dad's brother Jessie was doing more or less the same thing with his gry. This was a man who had not an ounce of fear of grys. By clicking his teeth he could get them to do almost anything. He would take bets on what his grys could do as well and make his pockets jingle. We enjoyed standing watching and taking in everything going on around us. For the next few days that's mostly what we would talk about, our grand day at the fair.

Getting bored with the grown-ups, we began to follow a group of young Travelling boys as they tried their luck on the stalls, trying to win coconuts and shooting the guns.

'Hey, Kalub, will you win me one of they dollies?' I begged.

'I'll sure try, our little Maggie,' he laughed.

'Bet you I wins her one first,' shouted young Tommy, so the bet was on. Did they two dinalows win me a doll? No they never – only lost their vonger to the fair mush.

'It wasn't meant to be,' our Alfie told me. 'But when I'm big I'll get you one.'

We soon lost interest in the boys who had won nothing and lost face to each other, so we moved on. We watched the big, brightly coloured dobby horses go round and round and the riders shouting out in glee to each other. We would have loved to join them, but we'd been warned not to get on any of the rides without me Mam or Dad there and that put the tin lid on that idea. Still, the lights and music were something to behold – just wait till dark and it got better still.

'Oh doughty, they two is gonna catch it.' Our Alfie was pointing out two lovebirds, tangled up in each other's arms. 'If me Aunt Kizzia spots them, she'll mour the pair of 'em.'

Sure enough, there cuddled up was young Jimmy and Britie, whose families was not on the best of terms right now. This could make the sparks fly if they got caught together.

'Come on, let's see what's happening back on the green. Bet me Dad can't stand. He'll be as drunk as a fiddler by now.'

As it happened, most of the Travellers were three sheets to the wind. Me Mam was giving them one of her old Devonshire songs:

A stepmother was brought home to me
who beat and kicked me to the floor
Every time I mention mother dear.

So you need not laugh because I cry
I have been lonely since my mother died

Friends and comrades turn on me,
they turn on me because I'm poor
So you need not laugh because I cry.
I've so been lonely since my mother died.

My Terry drives his horse Sunny in convoy round the lane.

As we watched, the tears fell from her yocks. It was a song she sang in honour of the mother she could not remember and when she sang this song, she once told us, she felt that her mother was nearby, listening to her. And, indeed, she had a stepmother who she never got on with when she was growing up. She's very deep thinking, is me Mam, and a very feeling woman. There's some who wouldn't help a lame dog over a stile, but not me Mam. She wanted to help everybody. And we chavvies was her very life, her pride and joy (and the same goes for me Dad too, of course, that goes without saying).

It was fun alive on the green – it was all going on. Wagons were being emptied, having been chopped out or sold. Bedding, pots and pans were spread out on the grass, ready to be packed in the new wagon. Young foals were running around between mares kicking up their heels, and out-of-breath boys were running other mares up and down in front of a large group of Travelling men who were bidding against each other for one or t'other of the horses. Traps and trolleys were pulled out on show to await new owners. Whips and driving harnesses were changing hands.

The wicker man, a basket-maker, had his baskets and hampers spread out for sale and, I might add, he was doing kushti business. He had a few hawking baskets kept back which had been made to order and were waiting to be collected and paid for.

There was a stall selling pretty ware – cups and plates – that was full of buyers too. And a gorgie woman who had learnt to make the black full pinnies and front pinnies was selling to the Traveller women. Pinnies has been a part of our everyday wear for many generations. They can be seen in old photographs as far back as our photographs go and in some families are still worn today. But the one doing the best trade was the pot man. He had every size of black cooking pots, kettles and teapots and the women craved them. We'd see them dragging their men over and shaming them into buying a pot or kettle – for shaming their men was the only way to get one or two much sought after pots. Then the men, who had been more or less forced to buy, would end up bragging about what they had bought their women. This in turn would shame others to do the same – it was a well thought out plan by the womenfolk and worked a treat. Cunning as foxes, some of these little women, but so long as it worked they all gained one way or another.

Hundreds of the local gorgies came to the fair, enjoyed a kushti day out and got themselves entertained by the Travelling families. A few nosy women would ask for a peep in the wagons and look surprised at how clean and pretty the insides were. How they thought we lived is nobody's business. I think they thought they might see a pigsty. It was as if they expected the wagons to be dirty and smelly, that's the way they thought we were. I think they were taken aback by how clean and fresh smelling these wagons were. We always watched their reactions if we let them view inside our wagons, for the bedding was clean and colourful, the lace curtains as white as snow, the little queenie stoves blackleaded to perfection and the floors as clean as tabletops. And if they poked around the tailrack, the pots and pans were as clean as new pins. So, yes, they did have a surprised look on their faces, much to the pride of the owners of these beautiful wooden wagons.

The gorgie men was much took by our coloured grys – and a display by one of our grys pushing back or turning a wagon on the soft command of its owner was well worth watching. Our men would show off the way their grys stood to be shod: 'Pick 'em up, Kit,' and on command the gry would lift its hoof ready to have a shoe put on. This training is all done by being kind to your gry and giving it a titbit (such as a good handful of fresh grass) as a reward while the job is being done, plus a lot of quiet chat while rubbing their ears. Of course we have the odd ones that rear up or do the viper's dance, but by giving them confidence and petting they soon learn to stand still. It takes patience and kindness to break any gry, but once the job is done, they don't forget it.

All too soon it was dusk. The lights shone out more brightly, the music seemed to get louder, but it also signalled to us that the fair would soon be over for another year. So we had to make the most of the next few short hours. How they sped by when we were enjoying ourselves.

To our delight our Alfie picked up a ten-bob note. He was so pleased with it, the dinalow had to find me Dad and show it to him. Dad promptly took it off him and handed us sixpence each in return. So much for that then. We could have nearly bought the fair with a ten-bob note; it was a lot of vonger in them days. Oh well, it was a kushti feeling while it lasted. Our loss, me Dad's gain, as they say, but we knew the next time to stay right away from me Dad if we found any vonger on the fairground.

I enjoyed seeing the faces of young and old lit up by the coloured lights round the rides and stalls. To us it was like fairyland, it gave you this lovely feeling inside. We had to grab every minute of the fair to savour later on in bed or on the morrow when we would be travelling

*My Terry and Steve Cooper breaking in Steve's trotting horse. A favourite pastime
for these two.*

long miles away from this place of happiness. It was a truly happy place
where children could be just that – children – for a whole day, running
around full of delight and not picking peas or sitting on the side of a
hop crib working all day.

Our way of life never gave us many full days off, for our lives
consisted of being on the move or working on the land or going out
hawking. People think because we chavvies worked from very young
that it was bad for us. This is not so. Everything we did – hawking or
field work – was a united family thing. It was family life and, if
anything, it put us on the right road to working and earning our own
living when we had families of our own. Gypsies are not work-shy. But
when we did take a day off it was to be fully enjoyed.

I'm now in my seventieth year and I still associate fairs with my
childhood. Soon I will be going to Priddy Fair on the Mendips in

Somerset, close to where I live. I shall find a spot to stand on the green and in me mind's yock I'll replace today's fair with them old fairs of years gone by. I shall visualise the old, long-dead Travellers with their wagons and grys pulled on this very same village green, wheeling and dealing, some staggering in lush, some giving the few old songs an airing and step-dancing on toes and heels. (Our old songs are being lost now and my aim this year is to record all the ones I grew up with afore they are lost for ever. Alas, we only hear them sung by the older generation at weddings and other happy gatherings now. The young ones are singing songs of today.)

I shall hear once again me Mam calling me back to the wagon, 'Peel a few taters, my Maggie, then you can go back to the funfair...'

I shall see them all as plain as day, then open me yocks to the fair as it is today – not a patch on the old ones. The green is now taken over by gorgie stalls, the sheep pens are long gone and the Gypsies are penned in a separate field up the road away from the fair with their grys, trailers and wagons and dared to drive or walk a gry out on the road. We've been pushed away from the fair, hidden in a field. Oh yes, they tell us it's a safety measure – and we have to pay twenty-five pounds or more to enter this field with our grys or turn round and go home. That's what's become of one of our beloved fairs, which we've supported for hundreds of years. This is only happening to Priddy Fair, because it's village-owned, which is a shame because this fair has always brought money in to the village. In a few short years there will be just the fun fair left. Once we stop taking horses this fair, like Glastonbury Fair, will die out. When Glastonbury stopped horse sales, within a few short years it was dead: all the local community have now is a few showpeople pulling on the outskirts of the town just for fair rides.

I'm glad to say that Bridgwater Fair, Stow on the Wold Fair and others are still going strong and have a good future.

Chapter Ten

Pride of the Road

ALL THIS TALK OF THE FAIRGROUND has brought a picture of our wagons to me mind. I know the wagons I grew up with off by heart – you might say inside and out. I'll tell you about them all, from my knowledge of travelling and stopping with them. We'll look at each wagon for its beauty and size and above all usefulness.

I'll start off with what we used to call the 'King of the Road', the Reading. This was one of the tallest wooden wagons to be built. I travelled with a good many of these Kings of the Road. Back then they were owned by the more well-off Traveller man – or I should say family.

This wagon was viewed with envy by many of my community – it stood out above the rest on a par with the Burton. It was built of high-quality wooden panels and had skylight windows in the roof which made it stand out. This wagon was very expensive to build and only the best wood and metals was used in the building of it. There was nothing plain about the Reading: above the door at the front and also to either side was wood carved in the shape of bunches of fruit such as hanging grapes or apples or the odd head of a horse. There was also carving inside the wagon around the stove, which was situated to one side. The frame of the two-berth bunk bed and the cupboards were also carved to perfection. Cut-glass mirrors hung over the fireplace. Even the glass in the skylight was etched. All in all this was a fine wagon, topped off with fancy lace curtains, good quality bedding and fine bone china.

Readings were taller than the Barrow Tops or Open Lots and had no sheeting or canvas on them apart from a piece to keep the tailrack dry in bad weather. They were built on a fancy trolley with higher wheels on the back end than the front which gave it a stately look. The wheels had spokes and a vellie (the vellie is the centre of the wheel which the wooden spokes are fitted into) set within a thick iron band. The flatbed trolley boasted a turntable kept well-greased for turning in tight corners. The living quarters were built up high with windows on all sides, including in the door and back end. Added to the skylights, that made for plenty of light inside.

The foreboard was wide enough for the driver to sit comfortably on. The sharves were wide and long – they had to be for it took a good strong horse to pull these early-made wagons. A pretty iron step was added to make getting in and out easier. Normally a set of wooden steps would be made to fit in between the sharves, but these could be an added burden and were not always carried on our travels.

These wagons were painted to a very high standard. It took a good painter to paint a wagon in the particular style we liked. If the builder couldn't paint it he would employ someone who could.

When this wagon was out on the road with a pair of coloured horses in the sharves, it was a pretty sight and brought many an envious glance, for it stood out among all the other wagons around it. I'm lucky enough to own one of my own now – well, I did own it until a few months ago, when on the passing of my beloved Terry, my husband, I gave the Reading to my son Jason and my old Barrow Top to my son Michael. But both wagons are still on my site for me to enjoy and my sons to take care of, and I am happy in the knowledge that they will remain here for years to come.

My Terry and our son Jason. Terry sold the pickup to Jason when he could no longer drive it because of his illness.

The early Burton wagons were not known for their prettiness. They were bulky and plain-looking, but once up the steps the inside took some beating. The carvings were outstanding – the bed frame and even the inside of the roof was all carved. Round the fireplace were bunches of fruit or horses' heads and all painted to perfection. In his later years my brother Robert owned one of these very early Burtons – I believe it dated from the 1870s. We so enjoyed sitting in it. He sold it some years ago when he retired through ill health, but the tears rolled down his cheeks as it was winched on a low-loader and driven away. It was a big part of his life but needed someone younger to give it TLC. These wagons need to be repainted every couple of years.

The later Burtons, on first sight, resembled the Reading. They was much sought after by wealthy Travellers, who took much pride in

My brother Robert with Danny and his son delivering the old Burton wagon.

owning one. These wagons also had cut or etched glass and was carved throughout like the Readings.

The Barrow Top: what a grand little wagon this is. It is built on a flatbed trolley and consists of a set of rounded bows which are then covered by a green canvas. It has windows on the back and in the door. Inside it has everything that the big wooden wagons have, only on a smaller scale. Instead of a cooking range it has the little ornate cast-iron queenie stove for heating. Barrow Tops were the most popular wagons on the roads and affordable to have made.

The Open Lot was also a Barrow Top wagon. The only difference was that it did not have a wooden door. Instead, the canvas cover came right round and laced up in the doorway. The inside was laid out the same:

My little Kite covered in snow.

bunk bed, queenie stove and lots of little cupboards. It had a window at the back end.

The Square Bow is the wagon I was born and brought up in. We loved this wagon. It was a touch wider than the Barrow Top, being built on a wider flatbed trolley, which gave extra room inside, and was popular with bigger families. It had very little in the way of carvings, just a bit on the door and tailrack. Like the Barrow Top, the Square Bow was very popular and much treasured by families. It was a familiar sight on the roads. I can remember it outnumbered the Barrow Tops or any other wagon in my younger years, at least in the area we travelled in. When I think of our travelling way of life, it's always the Square Bow that springs up in me memories.

The Kite was a small, wooden-built wagon, very unusual, and so very pretty and eyecatching. The shape was in the form of a child's kite – wide at the top and narrow at the bottom, with everything you needed built inside. I have a Kite and I love it. It's a rare one from the 1870s with thick, old, iron-bonded wheels, higher at the back than the front. Inside there's a tiny, very pretty and ornate bunk bed with cut-glass shutters and there's a cut-glass mirror over the fireplace. It's my prize possession but is in dire need of a set of new wheels which I will give it this year. Then it will last a few more generations and give more pleasure to whoever inherits it in the future. If I could be buried in me Kite I would lay in perfect peace.

There were other wagons on the roads, such as the Ledge and the Brush wagons, and places such as Evesham and Kent, I believe, made their own types too, but I would not recognise these. I only got to know the ones I shared the road with. I do remember that every so often we would buy a little squareish baker's wagon to be repainted and used as an extra bedroom. Flatbed trolleys were much in demand too, and traps that was sometimes used by the women to drive themselves out hawking. Anything with wheels on we made use of – even the baby pram was used to carry the many gross of clothes pegs round the doors, saving the women from having to carry them miles in baskets over their arms.

Each wagon was given its own personality by the family that owned it. The men took charge of the outside, seeing to repairs and painting. A lot of spit and polish went on their driving harness as well, to make it as good as their horse and wagon. Meanwhile, the woman of the family was in charge of the inside; it was her home on wheels. It went where the family went and she would put her stamp on it, just as me Mam did with hers. She would save a few secret pennies to buy little bits of lace, china (a bit of Crown Derby), brass cans or candlesticks to dress it up. Colourful plaid blankets would be folded up on the bed to show off her pretty bedding, and she would make her own frilly pillowslips and arrange her pillows on top of the blankets. The little queenie stove would shine like a button and you could eat off her floor. The perfume from the Mansion polish would waft out the door – even the floorboards would have been polished. The whole wagon was always as clean as a new pin.

Many a time when we were travelling and stopped in the middle of a town to shop, I have seen people pet our grys but they couldn't keep their yocks off the inside of the wagon – and they got a pleasant surprise at what they saw.

To round it all off, we chavvies was scrubbed and washed to match all the other possessions. All of a family's wealth was on show each and every day. And me Dad was blessed with a great deal of the same in owning a good sound wagon and a couple of sturdy piebald or skewbald horses to pull it (skewbald is red on white coat colour and piebald is black on white).

As you must have realised from my ramblings, wagons are still a big part of my life. I get such pleasure from looking at the shapes and paintwork, the different turntables under them. They're my oldest friends. They don't answer back or need feeding, just a bit of tender loving care inside and out.

I often think now, as I let me mind wander back to those days, how we must have looked to other people as we travelled along the roads from one stopping place to another: wagons in a long line – Barrow Tops and Square Bows, with a Reading here and there, and the horses full of shine and colour. It's true you never see yourself as others see you. All we were interested in was our own way of life and getting work. We didn't want to bother anyone who didn't bother us, because our own company was all we wanted. But we must have made a pretty picture all the same – handsome wagons and handsome horses topped off by the colourful people with them.

As you have read in this book, history has not been kind to us Romanies, but still the stubborn cuss within us makes life go on. Back then when I was a child, happiness was sitting on the foreboard of me Dad's wagon, feet dangling between the sharves and singing a little song in harmony with him as we slowly travelled along the lanes.

Chapter Eleven

The Arrival of Winter

WE SET OFF TRAVELLING and left the fairground far behind us. We had to think of how to earn back the vonger we'd spent at the fair. By now it was October, too late to pick the hops and fruit up-country, so it was decided we would travel back to the Mendips and try a few farms for stone-walling or hedging.

Plans had to be made for the coming winter. It was agreed we would not go back down the Prince Lane, for our family was happy and all in harmony – which the old Granny could soon put a stop to with her bitter tongue. Instead, me Dad would visit the old couple on horseback.

We had met up with John and Ellen again and then we came across Dan and Leal – Dan was me Dad's baby brother. In those days me Dad's six brothers were all strapping fit and healthy young men, with the stamina to work till they dropped, but now, instead of looking for farm work, they changed their minds and we headed for the back lanes around Frome, past Shepton Mallet to the little village of Nunney, where we pulled in tight to the hedge because those back roads were narrow.

Everything was fresh after a shower of rain and we were made to get into our wellingtons otherwise, Mam told us, we could ketch our death:

'You chavvies come back yer. Get these boots on or you're sure to ketch yer death. Then you'll know it! Then fetch me a bundle of wood – I gotta boil out me coupons.'

These were the coupons in me Mam's ration book. Out come the Parazone bleach as she waited for the kettle to boil. With the bleach you could get rid of the blue marks that the shopkeepers stamped on the coupons to show they'd been used. The stink of bleach would spread right up the lane: Ellen and Leal were up to the same tricks too. They also had small chavvies who needed that bit extra as well.

The three men had plug-chained their grys and watered them at a farmer's trough in a nearby cow field. The grys were now snatching mouthfuls of grass and taking a hard-earned rest. With luck we would not be discovered in the lanes for a few days, but just in case me Dad took a wheel off the wagon and hid it under a sheet. If the gavvers come, that would be our excuse not to move – a broken wheel being repaired. This ruse had been used many times afore and usually worked quite well.

The long summer days were behind us and the year was on the turn. The hedges were heavy with autumn fruit. The elder was thick with juicy deep-purple berries which we would pick for me Mam, some to make dye out of and some for medicine. Here and there a late elderflower was still in bloom and this we reached by using a long peg stick with a crook on the end. Mam would dry them and put them in a little muslin bag to make our wagon smell fresh. The blackthorn was now covered in very bitter blue-black berries which we would gather to add to the cough mixture – they cut through phlegm on the chest. Also we would sell them to housewives who used them to make sloe gin. Picking them was a tedious old job because they don't grow in bunches like most berries but have to be picked separately from between the thorns that can rip off your skin. But they brought in a few pennies.

The hawthorn bushes were covered in bright red berries hanging in bunches. They were of little use to us so we'd leave them as winter feed for the birds.

Hazelnuts were gathered up, some to sell to the shops as Christmas fare but most we would eat as we picked them or crawled around under the bushes to gather the slip-shells – those are the bronze-ripe nuts that have fallen out their shells onto the ground. It was a fight between us and the squirrels, though really there were plenty for all of us.

Me, our Alfie and Robert would wander away up the lane nutting – picking some for us and some to sell. Once on this game we would spend hours at it, it was so enjoyable. We could be tracked up the lane using the broken shells, but we were still given praise for the nuts we brought back. In just a few days we could fill me Mam's hawking basket right up. The shopkeepers would weigh them and pay by the pound – it was the same with the blackberries and mushrooms we picked as well. We'd get up at the crack of dawn to pick the young new mushrooms, putting the ones for the shops in a separate basket so as not to bruise them.

Me Mam's little store of nuts would be shared out on Christmas morning. Walnuts were one of our favourites and we knew if there were any trees in the area we were travelling close to. The shops went mad for these nuts, as did we. We would pick up the fallers then beat the branches to get more. There's an old saying: *'The more you beat a woman and a walnut tree, the better they be'*. I wouldn't know about that, for when me Dad beat me Mam she would lay in wait and get her own back on him.

We collected loads of rosehips for me Mam as well, to make the base for her cough mixture. And a few housewives would buy them for the same reason. We only picked the apples we could use as we had no way of storing them, but we also sometimes picked up fallen apples for the farmers who made cider. They paid us by the sackful – it was back-breaking work but we all pitched in to do it, men, women and chavvies. It was work and not to be passed up; any work, hard or soft, got done.

As you can gather, we Romanies made the most of what nature provided us with. It was all free with help from the old gal herself,

Mother Nature. All these memories come flooding back to me at the sight of the autumn hedgerows. It's a time in my life not easily forgotten.

October was also the wooden flower season. Me Dad and his two brothers would sit round the yog whittling dozens of beautiful chrysanthemum heads from that grand helpful bush the elder while we walked off to beg an armful of evergreen privet to marry them onto. This would start us off, for each day we would pick the privet for the morrow.

Afore we went out calling we had our own fry-up with a panful of button mushrooms added to the thick slices of bacon and fried crusty bread. People can be so lazy – the nuts and mushrooms grew all round these villages, but people would rather pay for them than get out and pick their own. Still, it brought bread to our hamper for us to do all these things so they could be as lazy as they liked.

Our flowers took some time to shift. We walked miles to other outlying villages, staying away from the town of Frome. We knew there were a large number of Traveller families that stayed in the Frome area and we had to respect the fact that we were on the edge of their patch. I say a 'large' number – around twenty-five to thirty families had made this area their base and seldom left it. Part of this group had been stopping on the same piece of land for many years and in the Fifties this was turned into a local authority site which the families paid rent to stay on. They're still there to this day.

Some days later we shifted on to Warminster, another area well known to me Dad's family, again collecting berries and nuts and mushrooms to sell. The weather was damp and getting colder; our little queenie was kept burning in the wagon to keep any damp out. Every day we hawked wooden flowers and clothes pegs and I was more than pleased to be dressed up warm and be part of this hawking group.

Our next stop was Westbury – just a few days here then on to Trowbridge. All our plans for the winter had been scrapped: we was having a kushti run on hawking. Then we took a detour around Bath, coming out on the toll bridge, known as the Sixpenny Bridge, at Bathampton. It cost sixpence for each wagon to cross, which made our men rear up. 'Bloody one and six,' they grumbled.

By November we were past Chippenham and pulled into a lane near Devizes. Here we met me Dad's other brother Jessie and his family. Our convoy was growing bigger. Now there were five wagons because Jessie had two (one was for his gals to sleep in). He was rich indeed, John told him.

'Yes,' he answered, 'things have had to change now me wenches is getting older. They've outgrowed me own wagon.'

'This is as far up as I intend to travel,' said me Dad. 'If we is to find a farm to take us on, we best split into two lots.'

'So you don't want me with yis, then?' said Jessie, taking umbrage.

'You, my brother, is off yer head. Just dick at the number of grys we got a-tween us. You got four and we three two each – who's gonna take that lot in for a start?'

'He's right,' said John. 'I'll hook up with you, brother,' he said to Jessie, 'and our Dan can go with our Lenard here.'

'Fair play,' said Jessie, 'I never reckoned on the grys. But we'll have a few days together afore we shifts on.'

For once, all were in agreement: there was too many of us travelling together; it made more sense to split up. After all, it was the grys they was worried about, with the long winter ahead.

After we'd split off, me Mam wanted holly and moss fetched to make the holly wreaths. One or two landowners let the men trim a few holly bushes while we chavvies gathered moss to bind round the homemade hoops that formed the base for the wreaths. These were made out of old man's beard, a wild plant. It was easy to cut and make the hoops out of and there was plenty of it. We had tried a few florist shops but they swore they had no wire wreath hoops to spare – which had meant we had to make our own. But it was easily done – nothing could put a damper on me Mam's plans once her mind was made up.

This was a job we could all join in with. As Leal couldn't get the hang of making a wreath, her job was to bind the moss to the hoops. Me and our Alfie picked off the holly to be placed in bunches round the mossed hoops, while the rest of the chavvies kept the yog in wood to keep us warm as we worked. This was family at its best, all working towards Christmas.

Soon the wreaths were being stacked face to face, like a jam sandwich, so the mice and birds couldn't pinch the holly berries and leave them colourless. The bunches of berries were dotted all round the wreath with variegated holly to make them stand out against the dark green holly used to make up the wreath itself. It's the bright red berries that set off the finished wreath and ketches folk's yocks.

Some people add ribbons and hang them on their doors, but most end up in cemeteries out of respect for the dear departed. Which was the reason they were made: wreaths belong in cemeteries, to our way of thinking, because they are connected to death.

We made dozens of these wreaths and they took little hawking to get rid of them. Some of the shops, such as butchers, wanted to take the lot in one go, they were so sure of selling them.

The big day was looming ever closer. What would we get given *this* Christmas? Our Mam had told us about the Father Christmas visiting all the chavvies and we had believed her every word. She was a great believer in keeping up traditions and gave us a little magic to look forward to.

It was going to be a snowless Christmas. Me Dad's nose could not smell any in the air as we took the last of the holly wreaths together with bunches of holly and mistletoe to the shops. It was a joy to stand and look in the seasonal windows of the little shops. The windows was cold and frosty on the outside but others afore us had rubbed it off so they, like us, could gaze in. In the grocer's cottonwool had been pulled and thinned out to make a snow scene: tins of corned beef was stacked up among a few Christmas stockings full of knick-knacks for children. There was an iced Christmas cake with a green frill running round it and a Father Christmas and a red robin perched on the top, plus a few boxes of pretty crackers. Oh I would have liked a cracker to pull, knowing full well it would be currants or apples to make puddings that me Mam would be buying instead. And there, right in the middle, lay a display of white sugar mice and a jar of bullseyes.

Oh well, I thought, let's await the coming of the old Father Christmas – that's if he can find us in the lane.

On to the butcher's shop. He had a few gooses hung up and some pheasants and chickens – all still in their feathers. Me Dad and Dan had spied where a few pheasants were to be found and they had booked them up for our Christmas dinners – but we only ate fresh meat caught on the day of cooking, so *our* dinner was still out there enjoying life.

The cold weather was well and truly set in. Dan and me Dad had got a job sweding, not out of choice – it was all there was to be had. Sweding was a job we passed up if possible, but beggars can't be choosers. It was work and had to be done, for the sake of our grys and pockets. Sweding was a bad old job to take on for, more often than not, these swedes would be frozen hard in the ground. The farmer would provide very sharp long knives or choppers to chop them out the ground and then top and tail them. There was no health and safety in those days: if one of the men cut themselves bad it was down to them. This could and did happen at times – working in frozen-solid fields cutting out frozen-solid swedes with hands and feet so cold they could not feel them, accidents did happen as they worked with the sharp tools.

Christmas Day dawned icy cold. We had hung our socks up on the front of the wagon – and the next morning found them half full of the hazelnuts and walnuts we had picked months back, oh and a sugar mouse, but it was grand. We were more than pleased with what we got (being a year older and wiser than the Christmas before).

Pheasant was missing off our Christmas menu because me Dad and Dan had been given several young cock birds by the farmer who they were to start cutting swedes for the day after the morrow. The two men had managed to get themselves in the kitcherma last evening and were not the brightest sparks this morning.

'Oh me poor old head,' cries Dan.

'Dan, go fetch me some wood. That'll clear your poor old head,' says Leal. 'You should've fetched it yesterday. Now you got no choice – no wood, no dinner.'

'Who's worried about dinner? I ain't had me breakfast yet.'

So at it they two went. She was trying to punish him for going off drinking, because in fact we was sharing one yog and had plenty of wood stacked up. He never noticed *that*, he only knew he had a hangover. But Leal wanted him to suffer for his sin; she would not let up – and it come to pass that he ended up stretching her out for the count.

Oh doughty, now me Dad's gonna upset me Mam, I thought to meself.

'Well, Vie, now you knows what to expect if *you* starts cutting any capers.'

'Yea, my Len, and dick at that boiling kettle. That will be *your* match an' master if you starts on me today.'

Dan told me Dad to let it drop – me Mam had done nothing to warrant a row. It was *his* woman who had made the row, she who was just getting to her knees, not knowing what day it was – and her yocks all but closing up on her.

'Happy Christmas morning, everyone.' I thought.

We had double the taters, cabbage and carrots to peel – poor Leal could only fumble her way through preparing the dinner. As Dan's fist had caught her right between the two yocks she could dick nixis (nothing). Oh he was real sorry, did he not just say so? But her answer, if Dan had done as she said, would have got him and his Mum locked up. She had told him to go fuck his old mother.

'You say that about me an' me Mum again, Leal, and I'll beat you till you pisses yourself.'

'It wouldn't be the first time, Dan. But remember I'm in your country – just you wait till you'm in mine, among my people, and me brothers are there.' True, Leal was a Hereford Traveller gal and was away from her family.

Me Dad, seeing me Mam throw down the bowl of carrots, knew it was time he stepped in and put a stop to a row that was getting out of hand, before his spitfire of a woman started on Dan. Because he knew me Mam would not stand by and do nothing if Dan set about Leal again. He had already hit her once, now end of.

'Let's fetch that wood,' me Dad nudged Dan. 'Come on, let they two cool down a bit, eh? Women will make themselves out to be a woman…' (In the Gypsy community women seek to prove in various ways that they are 'real women'. A woman may feel that her hard working life or the number of children she has produced or the fact that she is not afraid to answer back to her man marks her out as a 'real woman'. So to make out that your wife only *thinks* she is a woman, even as a joke, would be bound to provoke her.)

If me Mam had not heard me Dad make that last comment all would have been well. But she did and it cost the lot of us our Christmas dinner. The cocks flew one way – which pleased our juckles. Taters, cabbage and carrots went the other. Pots were kicked off the yog.

'Violet, I'm a-warning you,' shouted me Dad.

'And I'm warning you two brothers. Think you kin walk all over me, do you, Lenard? Well try walking over me brother Bobby. I'm sending for me brother.'

'Send for all your lot and Leal's too,' he hollered.

Me Mam's brother Bob Small outside his tent.

Well, Merry Christmas, everyone. Hope you enjoy your dinner because the juckles have had ours, I thought to meself as I bit the head right off me sugar mouse.

The two men walked off, but me and our Alfie knew it was not because me Dad was fret of me Mam's brother. Oh no, it was because

113

he would have beat the shit out of her, and then she would have cut his driving harness to pieces and anything else she could lay her hands on of his. No, better let her cool off for a bit. He was beginning to get the gist of me Mam, having lost that many sets of harness in the short few years he had had her. It made him stop to think – and, after all, she had done no wrong, it was they other two objects who had started it off.

After the men had left, me Mam called Leal out.

'Leal, I stuck up for you just now and what thanks do I get? Me and me man rowing, me chavvies got no grub, the juckles ate the cocks and you sat round the yog warming your minge. You best get a bundle of that wood there and light your own yog. Keep away from me.'

'I can't dick to light a yog, my Vie,' she cried. 'Me yocks is all swelled up.'

'Then feel the way,' says me Mam, 'and keep out me road.'

'You is gonna pack up and leave us, ain't you, my Vie? I know you is. Don't, my Vie, he'll take me back to his family, I gins he will.'

'Leal, I've had more than me fair share of Lenard's lot. Me and my chavvies is sticking it out on our own from now on – we travels with nobody else. So make the best of your own road – and get out me sight.'

'Well,' said our Alfie to me, 'it's true what me Mam says: every time she gets with me Dad's lot, she gets hit and knocked about. They makes trouble for her. But just you wait till I grows up – then they'll have it. So let's start packing up: her mind's made up. She'll go whether me Dad comes with us or not.'

And so things changed yet again. Me Dad too thought it best we split up – so, leaving Dan to cut the swedes, we pulled off the lane. The men were on speaking terms but not the two women.

Chapter Twelve

Heading into a New Year

BOXING DAY SAW US heading towards Bath again. It was rare for us to travel over the Christmas season, but needs must, as they say. After me Mam and Dad started speaking again – well, grunt at each other to start with – we ended up back in the Trowbridge area and me Dad managed to get us on a lonely old farm (with miles to walk to a shop). The farm was run by a brother and sister who we had not worked for before, but they turned out to be nice people. The mush we rarely set yocks on, but the sister was very helpful and took a shine to me Mam's clean ways – and me Mam thought her a very clean person as well and was glad enough to buy fresh-baked bread off her. Most days this woman would bake or make cheese and turn the cream churn. That was her daily life on the farm, making the provisions both for the farm and to sell on. I loved the smell of the fresh bread being made and the thump-thump of the dough as the woman beat it on the big old flour-covered table. And like many of our lot, I liked the smells of the farm, the scent of warm fresh milk straight from the cows, the smell of chickens and manure all mingled together.

Our two grys were being fed on meadow hay, plus Dad was getting a few shillings to make his pocket jingle. Me Dad's job was a bit of everything – hedge-laying and logging, with the odd day cleaning out the cow stalls – whatever needed to be done. We chavvies was given the task of feeding the chickens and collecting the youries (eggs), but we was not allowed to go near the big, fat spotted pigs. Me Dad gave us a dire warning on this and the farmer mush told us the same: if we fell in the wet slushy slurry they might bite us or crush us, not out of malice but ignorance.

All in all, we was kept busy going about our daily tasks on the farm. It was bitter cold and we dressed up warm to go out with me Dad on the farmer's big hay wagon to fetch the logs back to the farm from way across the fields. Throwing the logs high up onto the wagon bed kept us warm.

'You chavvies best look out your wellingtons when we gets back – there's snow in the air, I can smell it.'

There's me Dad's nose off again, up in the air, twitching away. But he's not often wrong. We laugh and tell him his nose could be his fortune.

The big Shire horse stands stock still as we run round chucking up the logs. It's very used to working in the fields and in harness, so standing still is one of its pleasures, I should think. The Shires are built much bigger than our cob-bred grys and pulling a heavy weight is no problem. These giants are so good-tempered and quiet to work with, but me Dad finds them slow and sluggish, not his kind at all.

Once ready to get the load back to the yard, Dad tells us to run on ahead to keep warm and we hear the click of his teeth as he shouts, 'Gid up, gid up,' and rambles his way back to the farm behind us. Not that the Shire needs much prompting, he knows the way better than we do. He was born and bred on the farm – the farmer has four of these big, beautiful animals, all working the land, pulling the ploughs and the high hay wagons, the chain-harrows, all the machinery needed to keep the farm rolling along. But if me Dad is right about the coming weather, these grys will get a long rest from their daily tasks.

Me Dad's prediction come true the next night, as we sat round the yog eating shussy stew. Soft flakes of snow began to fall, which brought smiles to the faces of us three older ones. We loved the snow and couldn't wait for it to pitch thick on the ground. The wireless (which we often listened to) gave out a warning of heavy snowfalls, prompting me Dad to tie a canvas sheet round the bottom half of our wagon to make a warm, dry place where our two juckles, Bizzie and Spider, could get in out the snow. And he kept a heap of dry kindling wood in there as well, to start the yog on a morning. We had a couple of bags of coke which we used in the little queenie stove to keep the wagon warm. Wood for the outside yog was no problem – the farmer mush supplied us with that. So, in other words, we lot was as snug as a bug in a rug, come what may.

And come it did. The next morning the snow lay crisp and deep, the tree branches bending with the weight and the hedges glittering in the morning light with a million diamonds. The roofs of the outbuildings and farmhouse were covered in thick newborn snow. It was a picture which took our breath away on first sight from the doorway of our wagon. Nothing can compare with this untouched, unspoilt first fall of snow.

Me Dad had the yog well alight in last night's fireplace, although it had been wet and soggy because the embers had melted the snow as it fell on them. Me Mam had the kettle on and the frying pan sizzling away with thick home-cured bacon, the smell of which had brought us from our sleep. The farmer had lent us a wooden apple box each to sit on, so we could eat our meals on our laps. The heat from the yog made a nice, warm, dry circle around it for us to sit in. Oh what a fine world we lived in, all white and sparkling, and by the look of the sky and what me Dad's nose was telling him, more was to fall. This is a scene all they poor people in the big towns don't get a chance to see for themselves. For our little group, cut off from the village, it was sheer bliss, for we had stocked up in plenty of time, thanks to me Dad's nose. No worries for us this winter.

Thus we passed the coldest spell of that winter: the farmer mush and me Dad seeing to the animals, me Mam and the farm lady cooking and keeping the yogs going day and night, we chavvies having the time of our lives, playing, rolling and falling in the snow, getting wet and cold then drying off or changing clothes and going back out in it again.

But, come the end of February, we was ready to hit the tober once more. The farmer mush and me Dad had got on like a house on fire and he had asked us to return come next winter, which pleased us. Me Dad told him if we were in these parts we would. The lady of the farm gave us all the bacon, cheese and butter we would need on our journey and wished us luck.

Our two grys felt fresh and a bit collar-proud for the first couple of miles, then it was back to normal – heads up and pulling the weight of the wagon.

We had gone right through the four seasons and come out intact, to start all over again. Wild spring flowers would be picked and sold again. Pegs would be made and hawked off. Devizes May Fair would be travelled to and enjoyed by one and all. Once again the pea fields would have the Romani families picking their crops and the hop gardens would find us grumbling as we worked in the early morning mist. Wooden flowers by the hundreds would be whittled and dyed and sold round the doors. Hay making, plum- and apple-picking and every other job that came our way would be tackled and finished. This was how our lives ran, year in, year out.

Looking back, these bygone days pull at me heartstrings. I see me Mam and Dad as young parents again. Me old Granny (God rest the old dear) and me dear old Grandad are both so very clear in me mind's eye. But, alas, as I sit and write this, every one of me Dad's family, including him, is long gone to their resting place. The same goes for me

I grow me own hops at home so I can still do a bit of 'hop-picking' each year.

Mam and her family – a whole generation is now under the earth, but kept alive by memories.

It's meself and me two brothers and two sisters and many cousins that are the older generation now. My sons and *their* age group are today's Romanies. I have seen so many changes in my lifespan, both good and bad.

The old bender tents have been revived by the New Travellers – the young people that have chosen to leave dwelling houses and take to the roads. These people are not Romani but I guess they feel life is better out of dwellings.

The wagons that were exchanged for (motorised) trailers in the late Fifties are making a comeback – many of my community are returning to them, forced by today's social pressures. The lack of sites and pitches and the fact that living-in trailers and touring caravans are almost outlawed on the roads today means there is no peace for roadside families. They're constantly moved on and their caravans searched by the police. Sometimes families believe they'll get more peace if they travel in horse-drawn wagons and as more and more families who own wagons and horses use them to travel to traditional horse fairs we find they are staying out on the roads longer now than they did a few years ago, before returning to their touring caravans or unauthorised camping. But travelling in horse-drawn wagons has its drawbacks too, for with the huge increase in traffic it only takes a short while for vehicles on the road to form a long tailback behind the slow-moving wagons – and tempers soon flare. Today's society is far too fast for our old way of life and there's nothing we can do about it.

Trailers are also being exchanged for more and more mobile homes which are placed on private or authority-owned sites. But most families usually keep one touring trailer for the nomadic part of our lives, no matter where we live.

Our coloured grys are more popular now than they have been for years. There's a lot of good breeding taking place. I hope these grand old Gypsy grys will never die out – they was members of our old families and part of our way of life.

Wooden flowers and pegs can once again be bought at our traditional horse fairs, and black cooking pots and swing-handled frying pans are being snapped up there too. The old-style water cans have been brought back into use by many families, but now, instead of copper and brass, they're made of tin and chrome. It's kushti that so much of our history is making a comeback. My family, like all my race, is steeped in history. We Travellers are so well known for our land work, for horse-breeding and for making medicines and potions. We have the ancient skills of making a living out of the wild hedgerows, verges and woods.

I know our language, culture and traditions will thrive and be passed down through the coming generations because our love and regard for them are so deep-rooted.

Part of that culture was to marry our own kind, to keep our people pure Romani Gypsies as far as possible. Another reason to marry within Gypsy circles was to keep out the very people who in many cases had made our lives a misery – the gorgies. Gorgies were not made very welcome within our community when it came to marriage.

But being of a strong-minded nature, I knew I would not marry one of me own – if the day ever came for me to marry. It was not that I didn't love and respect me own people, because I did and still do, but the amount of control that, years ago, our men had over the women put me off for life.

I have cried at the sight of Mam's swollen-closed black yocks that she couldn't see out of for days on end. But she was made of strong stuff for a small person and she would lay in wait and get her own back, making me Dad pay dearly for his rough treatment of her.

Me Dad controlled me Mam, or tried to control her, but she lived up to her first name, which was Defiance. She would never give in. Yes, she had some beatings off me Dad. In fact as we were growing up I saw me Mam take many a beating at the hands of me Dad. She was a very stubborn woman who had been controlled by her father and stepmother when she was younger. Then, when she got me Dad, she found she had walked right in to another controlling situation. So she thought she had had enough of being controlled and she would rebel and stand up to me Dad in an argument. She got a reputation for sticking up for herself. If he beat her she would wait till he was asleep and get her own back: she would cut up his harness and then tell him not to beat her for something she hadn't done but to hit her now for something she *had* done.

When we travelled alone they rarely fell out, but once we met up with Dad's family trouble would brew. Me Mam's sisters-in-law would tell me Dad lies about her and he would believe them. Then me Dad would beat me Mam. But, God bless her, me Mam would wait till, one by one, she caught her sisters-in-law on their own and beat shit out of them. It would be their husbands, me Dad's brothers, who knew their women had told lies and who would stick up for me Mam against their own women, telling me Dad to leave her alone.

Me old Granny was the worst of all for she hated me Mam and was the cause of many beatings and rows. Yet years later, when the old woman was dying of cancer, it was me Mam who looked after her. Do you know what me Mam said as the old Granny lay a-dying? 'My Lenard, I lit me a candle to the devil, because your old mother was the devil itself.'

I suppose you could say that me Mam made a big impression on my young mind, for I knew that, like me Mam, I could not let meself be controlled. I was never going to be no man's punchbag or work horse. I was a person in me own right and that was how it was going stay.

Chapter Thirteen

Mixed Marriage

I HAD BOYFRIENDS FROM MY OWN COMMUNITY, lovely boys who took me to the pictures, which me Mam and Dad were happy about. But these same boys would criticise me for the clothes I wore, because now that I was earning I bought meself new clothes – shorter skirts, low-necked jumpers and high-heeled shoes – and wore more make-up, which they would tell me to wash off me face. And as for the job I had got meself in a factory, it would be, 'What do you want to work with they old gorgies for? You should be out calling with a basket on your arm, that's what you should be doing, my gal.'

I'd say to them, 'Well, hear me, I've called the doors all me life with a basket – I can get me 'living', as you call it, but I'm not now or ever going to be at your beck and call. I'll do the job I wants to do. You go your way – and I'll take me own road.' With any luck they would give me up as a bad job and leave me alone.

So I began to date a gorgie boy I met at work. When I say date, we ate our dinner together at work – I never saw him outside work. In the end I got found out and had to own up to me misdemeanour. Me cousin who worked in the same factory let it slip that I had a gorgie boyfriend. Now, if I had committed a murder the family would have supported me, but I had done worse in their eyes – I had committed a sin and I had to be sorted out: gorgie boys were definitely not welcome in my community. I was told I had to give up me job, that I would not be allowed out, even to go to the shops. I had to go back to staying at home, cooking and cleaning.

'I shan't, Dad, and I shan't give up me job. I pays you me keep every week. I'm seventeen not seven. I been working two years now, I ain't giving it up.'

Crack, I caught a back-hander across me face. 'Cheek me, my Maggie, and I'll break every bone in yer body.'

Me Dad had never hit me like this afore. It was a shock. But if I gived him best now my life as I'd got to know it would be gone. 'Well, my Dad, you'll just have to mour me.'

Our Alfie stuck up for me. 'Leave her be. Don't you hit me sister no more, Dad, I'm a-warning yis. She ain't done no harm. Leave her be.'

He took me outside and told me, 'Stick to your guns, our Maggie, you ain't done no harm.'

'Oh my brother, I shan't never marry one of our own. I'll leave home first. I'll run away, I will, my brother, I'll run away.'

'You would never do a daft thing like that. Leave it with me, I'll chat to 'em.'

Our Alfie warned me Mam and Dad that I could run away from home. Did they want that? I think this really frit them and they eased off me a bit. But I stuck in there and in the end they told me to bring him to their place at Keel's Hill (in the village of Peasedown St John near Bath – me Dad had bought a bit of ground there and they had made it their base from which to travel). So I did. Well, me Dad called him all the names under the sun, some very insulting, I must say.

The poor boy had ginger hair – so he was named the Ginger Pig by me family. I can't for one minute say I was in love with him, but this boy brought me some hard-earned freedom – and a taste of what it was like not to be criticised for the way I looked or what I wore. It felt kushti to go out just as I pleased. The only reason I was allowed out with this young man was because I had explained to me Mam and Dad that he was a good friend and looked out for me at work. It was not a love match in any way on my part, but I explained to me Mam that with him to protect me from harm I could see a bit of life. I was of an age when they had to give me some freedom and me going out with someone they could trust was better in their eyes than having me running wild with a bunch of gorgie gals. They never did trust the gorgie gals who would make silly comments about boys in front of me Mam and Dad when they called for me to go out with them. Those daft comments made me parents think that the girls led a bad life and went too far with boys – it brought no end of trouble for me. I was better off with the Ginger Pig!

This relationship would never have gone anywhere and we both knew it. One reason was that he was an only child and his mother had better things in mind for him than to end up with a Gypsy gal of all people. I knew he had his problems at home over our relationship, just as I had mine. He took me home to meet his parents: his Dad took it, well, okay, but the looks his mother gave me said it all. It was a shock for her to be entertaining a wild Gypsy girl in her own home – what would the neighbours think? And all the relations? I could read it all in her face.

Then I got a job in Bristol. I was now twenty years old and working in the Co-op tailoring factory at Brislington in Bristol (and the ginger boyfriend was overseas doing his National Service). To save all the travelling to work I was living with a girl from work and just going home at weekends. I was not going out with any boys, just working and spending weekends with me family. Life was running pretty smoothly for me, the family was as close as ever – in fact I felt they was proud of me; the gorgie boy was over the sea, much to me Dad's pleasure – well out of reach of his eldest daughter.

And that was when I met the man of me dreams – my Terry – so a Dear John letter flew across the water and probably made his mother very happy.

I kept me new man away from me family, not really knowing how he felt about me yet. We had been meeting for three weeks when he took me for a drink to a pub one evening. He was uneasy and I knew there was something in the wind.

'Shall we go?' he said, 'I want to talk to you.'

'That's alright,' I said, thinking he wanted to tell me it was over. Short but sweet.

He drove out to a layby just outside of Keynsham. And all the way there I was thinking to meself, 'Pity, I really liked you, and now it's over.'

But he took the breath right out of me body when he said he had loved me on first sight and would I marry him? Like a dinalow I just looked at him – then me mind went into top gear: there was trouble ahead. Oh my life, more trouble for me.

'Well, what do you say?'

'You know nothing about me,' I told him.

'I know I love you. That's all I need to know.'

'Look, Terry, I must tell you, I'm a Gypsy.'

'What's that, then?'

'I'm a Romani Gypsy. I was born in a horse-drawn wagon. Me family's Gypsies.' It turned out the poor lad knew nothing at all about Gypsies, so the word 'Gypsy' had no meaning for him. 'Look, Terry, your family won't accept me – and I can tell you now, my lot won't accept you.'

'It's not up to me family who I marries,' he told me. 'It's our life, not theirs.'

Oh doughty, I thought, my lot will make it their business. Just wait till the word wedding is mentioned – me Dad will beat him with his hat or his driving whip – which ever is closest at hand.

'Are you going to let your family rule and ruin your life?' he asked me.

Rule me life? Me Dad will *take* me life when this lot hits him, I cried inside. But I said, 'No, I won't let them. Yes, I'll marry you.'

He went wild. He was so happy it stopped me thinking about me family and the rows to come. We laughed and cried at the same time before he dropped me off at my mate's place.

Sleep wouldn't come. I was rehearsing how to tell me Dad. He would murder me stone dead. And me Mam, who had a temper like a boiling kettle, always ready to spit. Then there was the two boys, Alfie and Robert, who could fist-fight like professionals... Oh Lord, now you done it, Maggie. I went and talked it over with me friend, who could not for the life of her see me problem.

The next night Terry and me talked and talked about my culture and way of life. Instead of being worried by what he heard, he got fascinated and starting making jokes about us being chalk and cheese.

We began to make our wedding plans   it would have to be done on a shoestring. Between us we had about two hundred pounds. The marriage was to be booked in the register office in Bristol.

Then he took me home to meet the family. Not one problem – his Mum and Dad were fine with the idea of us getting married. They were used to him being away from home – he had only been home for a few weeks since doing his National Service, which he had served out in Aden and other far-off places.

We got the wedding date – 10th March – which meant that we would have met and married within six months. Now it was time I told my family – a case of shutting the gate after the horse had bolted – but there was no going back on me word.

I knew I was breaking with tradition and would really upset me family, so I had a heavy heart as I got on the bus to go home and break the news to me Mam and Dad. Also, I had to get written permission from me Dad afore I could get married. I was still only twenty and back then you had to have your parents' consent until you was twenty-one.

The bus seemed to speed along faster than usual as it took me to a heap of trouble. I didn't want to hurt anyone, but at the same time I had met a lad whom I loved dearly – he was my future, whatever it would bring.

The bus stopped up the top of Keel's Hill. As I walked down the lane, working out how to break me news, I felt as light as a feather. There was no feeling in me legs. When I entered the hut the family lived in their smiling faces greeted me.

'Oh, here's our Maggie come to see us. Sit yourself down – kushti to see you.'

'Move up, Robert, let our Maggie sit down,' said me Dad, so happy to see me.

He had wanted me to come back home to live, and each time they saw me their eyes searched for the suitcase that would tell them I was coming back into the family.

And all this time they're being so nice and kind to me, I'm thinking, 'Oh Gawd, how is I going to tell them?'

'Dad,' I says, thinking he would be the best one to start with, 'I got something to tell you. I'm gonna get married.' I just blurted it out. There it was – out. I had done it.

'Married?' me Mam asked. 'Is you in trouble, my gal?'

'No, Mam, I'm not in any trouble, but I'm gonna get married to a boy I met in Bristol.'

'A Traveller boy? Who is he one of?' asked me Dad, meaning which family was he from.

'No, Dad, he ain't a Traveller. He's a gorgie boy.'

'What, a fucking gorgie mush? Oh no, my Maggie, not a bloody old gorgie. You ain't marrying no gorgie mush – over me dead body.' There was tears in me Dad's yocks.

Then me Mam starts telling me she would rather see me dead than married up with a gorgie. Everyone was shouting at me at the same time. On and on they went at me: ain't our lot good enough for you, Maggie? You bloody little cow! Just look what I reared, a gorgie-loving

Traveller. What have I done in me life to deserve this? Over me dead body will I let you marry up with a gorgie mush…

Me Dad went wild. I really do think he could easily have wrung me neck, for I had been nothing but trouble to him for years. This was the second time I had broke his heart over gorgie boys.

I ran out the door, with the paper that I had been going to ask me Dad to sign clutched tight in me hand. I couldn't stick the pain I had brought on them and I couldn't bear me own. I felt I had lost me family and was not wanted any more. Was my Terry worth all of this, I was asking meself. I was no baby, I was twenty years old, but I felt as though I was turning me back on all me culture – and on me Mam and Dad, brothers and sisters. By now I had three sisters (Emily, Holly and Maralyn) and three brothers still living (Alfie, Robert and young Richard), having lost little Jess eleven years afore, so it was a big loving family I was giving up. Was it worth it? The question kept hitting at me as I walked out of their lives and back to the bus stop.

'Hang on, our Maggie,' I heard behind me. It was our Alfie. 'Wait, my sis.'

I stopped and waited for him, thinking he was going to knock me down in the lane, which I would not have felt as I was numb to me heart.

'My sis – you is me oldest sister. Don't do this thing to the old couple. Let's chat about it.'

'Alfie, my brother, I shan't change me mind. I'm getting married and that's that.'

'You always was a stubborn cuss,' he laughed. He asked me where and when it was to be, which I told him.

'He's a kushti man, Alfie. I thinks the world of him – and he me,' I cried.

'But what made you pick a gorgie of all people? You knowed it would bring you trouble,' he said, hugging me now. 'You know something, our Maggie, they two back there have let you have too much of your own way. Now I'll come back with you and get your bits of things, then you gotta come home.'

'No, my brother, I've picked the road I'm going to travel and there's no going back. I shan't change me mind, our Alfie. I know me Mam and me Dad hates me for it, but I gotta take me own road, I have, our Alfie.'

'I knows you better than you knows yourself, our Maggie, and I knows you means what you says, but you is me sister and I shan't turn me back on you. I don't like what you're doing but I'm still your brother.'

'You won't hit and knock me mush about, will you?' I asked him as me tears fell on the lane, me heart breaking wide open.

'No, I won't, but I can't say the same for me Dad. You've sent the pair of them off their heads. If your mush was here now, me Dad would mour him stone dead.'

'I knows that, and it means that, unless you finds me, I shan't see yis again,' I cried, 'but I'll miss the lot of you for the rest of me days.'

He held me close and then I caught the bus back to Bristol. I was full of pain and feeling like a lost sheep, well, a black sheep at least.

I had plenty of thinking time as the bus made its long winding journey back to the city. Had I done right? Should I kiss me mush farewell and go back home where I belonged? Would life with Terry work out for me? Could I stick not being a part of me family? So many things went through me mind. I was an outcast now and it didn't feel too good. I had lost all that I had held dear.

Me mush was waiting at the bus stop for me. He could see I was upset and he cuddled the life out of me. Was I ever pleased and relieved to see Terry waiting for me at the bus station. All the country buses ended their journey there so we couldn't miss each other, even if he had a long wait. There was a café inside where he could sit until he spotted my bus coming in.

'I'll make it all right,' he said, after I told him what had happened.

'I'm dead and buried to me family.'

'Then we'll start a new one.'

'But I wants me old one.' I cried bitter tears in his arms. 'And I wants you.'

'Look, Maggie, let's go for something to eat, then you can really explain the trouble and maybe I can talk to your family and make them understand.'

'Oh don't go near them, they'll kill you stone dead, I know they will. Promise you won't go near them.'

'All right, I promise. But Gypsies or not, they ain't allowed to kill people,' he laughed.

The poor blind fool thought it was a joke. He thought he could walk in and sit down and chat it over with me family, not realising I had committed one of the biggest sins in the Gypsy tradition: thou shalt not marry outside your race.

As me wedding day grew closer, I was not the happy bride I should have been. Me family kept creeping into me brain. My friends at the place I worked in tried hard with me. They made me a dress, had a whip-round and bought me many gifts, just as they did for their own. Terry and I found a flat to live in on St Marks Road in Bristol and our friends pitched in to decorate it. I made the Gypsy frilly lace curtains – at least I could dress the flat as a wagon inside and make it more like my kind of home. That made my Terry laugh and shake his head at me. You can't take the Gypsy out of a Gypsy, I told him, so don't try. True to his word, he never did – he loved me for being just me, as I did him.

Heavy storms lay ahead on our life's path. I knew right from day one my man would not be accepted within my family. We went out in his car one day and were driving round the countryside when I asked him to pull over and reverse back the way we'd come: I had spotted the top of a wagon and smoke rising over a hedge.

He stopped the car and asked what was wrong.

'Nothing's wrong, my Terry, but I want to show you first-hand who I am.'

'I can see who you is,' he laughed.

'No you can't, all you can see is me body. There's more to me. Much more. Drive up that lane there and stop when I tells you to.'

'Okay, anything to make you happy,' and he drove back along the lane till the wagon came in sight.

'Pull up by that wagon. I want to introduce you to some of my family.'

I must say, his face was a picture. If things hadn't been so serious, I would have laughed. We pulled in past the wagon and got out. I knew the couple in it well and had travelled with them and picked peas and hops with them many times.

'Hello, Uncle Eli, hello Aunt Esther.'

'Well, if it ain't our Lenard's gal Maggie. Kushti to dick yis, me gal. Set yerself down on that tin there. Esther, make a drop of sloppy [tea].'

His face changed when he saw who I was with. I waited for the talking-to to start.

'Right. Now, my gal, afore we gets any further, how come you is in a car with a mush? Yer Dad will mour yis, I'm telling you. You should know better. A gal your age should know better…'

On and on he went: Gypsy gals could never be alone with a man – Gypsy or gorgie. I had known this would happen and I wanted my mush to see for himself how we Gypsy gals were supposed to behave: how important to our good names it was that we not be alone with any man.

Then me Aunt Esther chucked the tea out the pot.

'They ain't a-drinking outta me cups. They ain't fit to drink out me cups.'

This, then, was the reaction of a close family friend – I had made meself unfit to drink or eat with my fellow Travellers, because I had become a loose woman – or gal, as they called me, by driving alone with this mush.

'I shan't tell yer Dad I seen yis, but don't come yer agin, Maggie. Getting us two in trouble with your family. You've done wrong by stopping at me yog.'

Now it was time for me to try and explain I was getting married.

'Uncle and Aunt, hear me out. The banns is in – we're getting married in a few weeks' time. And me Dad knows about it.'

'But that mush stood there is a gorgie mush, Maggie. Whatever is yer Dad a-thinking of, letting you get hitched to him?' Aunt Esther hissed at me. 'You'll put yer poor Mam in her grave with these carryings on. Now get going, get out me sight. I don't want you here.'

Lesson Number One for me mush: he was astounded to hear these people speak to me like they did – or as much as he could understand, for most of what was said was in Romani, but the body language said it all. It was threatening to say the least.

'Yes, my Terry, but I knew how they would react to me, being with you. And remember, they have known me all me life. They only spoke the truth as they see it.'

'What have they got against me? I've done no harm to you or them.'

'But they were not mad at you,' I told him. 'All the bitterness will be aimed at me. It's all my doing, in their eyes. It's not just my parents I've let down, but them too, in their eyes. My lot truly believes we should marry one of our own – they punish the ones who kick over the traces. And that's just what I've done, kicked over the traces.'

'So they'll make you an outcast, then?'

'Yes. I'm an outcast already. It'll be many years afore I'm back in the fold, if ever. It all depends on me Mam and Dad. If I can get them to take to you, at least the other Travellers will respect me Dad. He will lose face in their eyes, because of you and me.'

'My God,' he said, 'your lot is ancient.'

'Is you swearing at me family?' I asked, not knowing what 'ancient' meant.

'No, Maggie, I'm trying to understand where they're coming from. You haven't committed any major sin – we fell in love. What's so wrong with that?'

'Nothing, my Terry, we haven't killed anyone. But we can't rely on any help from the family, we must make the best of our road.'

He laughed and thought that was a funny expression, as he found many over the coming years.

Lesson Number Two. As we drove on I told him, 'Now you've stood round a fire by a Romani Gypsy wagon, listening to one of my people talking. And don't for one moment think he was enjoying himself – he wasn't. He talked a lot of sense to me, just as he was brought up to do. And I took no grudge against them for that. You saw the wagon, you saw how they live: that, my Terry, is how I lived all me life until a few years ago when me Dad bought Keel's Hill, where me family now live.

But if me Dad has his way, they could end up back on the road again, travelling like the family you just met.'

'Do your parents live in a wagon?' he asked.

'No, they live in a big hut with bedrooms in it.'

'Do they still travel?'

'Yes, they leaves the ground to go hop-picking and pea-picking and to go to things like horse fairs.'

'What do they sleep in while they're travelling?'

'A trailer,' I told him.

'A trailer? What's a trailer, then?'

'We call caravans "trailers".'

Then he surprised me by saying, 'That's a pity, Maggie.'

'Why?'

'Because I noticed your Uncle Eli's horses – they was grand.'

'Oh, me Dad's got horses just like Uncle Eli's. Why? Do you like horses?' I asked him.

'I do now,' he said.

'Well, I'll make you a promise. One day when we get on our feet a bit, we will have ourselves some horses. How's that?'

That's the sort of conversations we had. He was full of questions and wanted to learn about my way of life, which was so different from his own. He was properly interested.

I was very proud of my tall, slim, fair-haired mush with his bright blue yocks. I promised meself I would do all I could to help him understand my ways, to make his future road easier and lighten his load.

Our wedding day loomed – I say 'loomed' because I was concerned it would all go wrong or he would not turn up. But I had forged me Dad's name on the paper giving permission for me to get wed so we were all set to go.

The day itself came. I had stayed the night with me best friend Pat. It was at her wedding to Mike that I had met my Terry. We got very little sleep and were up bright and early. I couldn't eat a thing, only drink a cup of sloppy.

'Do you think he'll turn up to marry me, Pat?'

'He'll be there, don't fret so.'

But I did fret. I had a terrible feeling of foreboding – something was going on, something would happen.

Then the car come to take me and Pat to the register office. I saw there were two men in the car – and to my delight, then dismay, one of the men was me Dad.

'Oh my God, Pat, me Dad's out there. He'll kill me, I know he will.'

'Yes, Maggie, I know he's out there.'

'Oh, Pat, I'll have to hide. Don't answer the door.' I felt sick to me teeth and frit to death. There went me wedding day.

'Maggie, I knew your Dad would be here.'

'Why, Pat, why have you done this to me? I told you me family was against me marriage. Now there'll be ructions.'

'It was nothing to do with me. It was Terry and one of your brothers and my Mike. Your Dad has come to give you away.'

I went out to get in the car, feeling very sheepish – and ready to duck if me Dad's fist come my way. But he never spoke one word to me all the way to Broadmead. He talked to the driver and puffed on his fag, tipping ash over me while he was at it. When we pulled up there was all me family standing to one side – Alfie, Robert, me Mam, Emily, Holly, Mo (Maralyn) and Richard – I just couldn't believe me yocks. Every man jack of them was there. Even me cousin Willie and one of our Robert's mates was there.

In another group stood all my Terry's friends and family. Me Mam and Dad would not so much as look at me. To my mind, they had come to watch me defy them, which cut me like a knife – I could feel their pain at my having turned me back on me race. There was a thick atmosphere outside the register office. Me brothers and sister smiled but stayed where they were – there was no hugging and kissing me. I looked at my husband-to-be and thought, 'If we both gets through this day without ending up in hospital, we'll be lucky.' Then I told myself, 'If it happens, it happens. There's nothing I can do about it.'

We were all called in to the office. You could hear a pin drop, it was that quiet, then the registrar mush started the service. To this day my actual marriage is a blur – I have no romantic memories of saying, 'I do', only the bit about, 'Who gives this woman…?' and me Dad bellowing, 'I do'. 'Dear Lord, strike me dead afore me Dad does,' I remember thinking.

It was over – I was married. I was in a daze when me Dad made a speech to me there in the register office.

'You made your bed. If it gets rough, don't come running home to me. Your bed's made, now lay on it.'

He then turned to my Terry and said, 'If ever you beats or treats my gal bad, I'll kill you stone dead.' Then he walked out with me family behind him, leaving everyone there with their mouths hanging wide open. So far, so good. I thought they were off home and felt relieved.

We had a few pictures taken, some with me Mam and Dad who we discovered were still waiting for us outside. Then we were driven away to the reception at a hotel in Kingswood – I think my Terry's mates thought a fight would break out if they didn't get us out of the way sharpish.

Terry said to me, 'I never expected that – your Dad threatening me in the register office. And he's a big-built man, Maggie.'

It was the first time he had met me Mam and Dad or any of the family, apart from that little mush our Alfie, who had tracked my Terry down and got the family to the wedding. How he achieved it was never explained to me, but he loved me and tried to help me on my wedding day. I think he must have blackmailed my lot to get them there – otherwise there's no way me Dad would have come.

On entering the hotel I breathed a sigh of relief: my lot weren't there. They must really be on their way home now, I thought, thank God. The room had been done up by Terry's mates and their wives. It looked lovely and I began to relax for the first time that day. Then in trooped my lot and found themselves seats round the table. They had made a big effort to dress nice, I noticed as I took a quick look at them: me Mam looked pretty in her skirt and jacket and me Dad was smart in his long black funeral overcoat, which was a silent message to me: 'Dick at yer Dad, Maggie, I'm dressed for a funeral,' it said to me. 'I know how you feel, Dad,' I felt like saying.

But everything went off well. I had warned my Terry that if me Dad got heavy in drink we would leave pronto, but at the end of the afternoon me Dad and the boys invited us out to their local pub. Well, I wasn't asked but my Terry was. We was to drive out to the Beehive at Carlingcott and drink the night away. In fact the invitation was extended to all the wedding guests. What sly deeds was me Dad up to now, I wondered. Would this day never end?

First Terry and me went back to our flat. How well it had all turned

Our wedding day and the start of our mixed marriage.

out, my new husband said – 'After all your worrying'. Instead of enjoying our first hours together as husband and wife, we found ourselves discussing my family.

'I noticed how big your Dad was, Maggie, and his hands are like hams.'

'Yes, me Dad is a big sturdy feller. I've seen him put many a fighting man down with one punch. So beware of him, he hits first and asks questions after. You don't know him at all – his love for me, for all his children, can make his fists fly.'

'I'll never give him cause to knock me down over you.'

I knew he was sincere at that moment. He had a grand personality and a sweet temper and he was my brand-new husband. It was up to me to protect him from my lot – and I would, come hell or high water. He was me man, really mine now.

Later that evening a crowd of us went out to me Dad's pub. My man was bought a drink, but there was nothing offered to meself. Me Mam stayed in one room and I was relegated to the children's room, where they thought I belonged – with all the chavvies. I had been put in my place and I accepted it. I knew that if I went to the bar it would only bring me grief. I was given no wedding presents from my side, neither did I expect any, but little Mo gave me a pair of black cats which I still have to this day as a kushti luck charm.

During the evening me cousin Jessie turned up. He had no idea he had walked in on a wedding and was surprised to hear I was now married. He had met Terry in the public bar and now came searching for the bride. When he found me he made me go with him into the main bar.

'What's you hiding away for?' he asked. 'Is you ashamed or what?'

'No, I'm not ashamed, I'm a married woman now.'

'Then be one and come and show yourself,' he scolded me.

On our one-day honeymoon in Bournemouth.

'I don't want to upset me Dad,' I cried.

'He's upset any road, by the looks of him. Come on, come with me.'

So I found meself with the wedding guests, including my Terry's mates from Bristol.

'What are you going to have to drink?' Jessie asked me, rather too loudly, so that me Dad heard.

'I'll get her one,' said me Dad – he couldn't lose face. 'What do you want?'

Before I could reply he told the landlord to give me a glass of lemonade. Well, at least he'd spoke to me, even if it was through grinding teeth.

At last it was home time. I've never felt so relieved. As we drove back to Bristol my Terry told me that he had been warned yet again by me two brothers and me Dad about looking after me and treating me right – even me cousin had had a word in his ear.

The next day we drove down to Bournemouth for a day's honeymoon. We had our picture took walking along the seafront and ate fish and chips out the paper on a bench while we watched the waves roll in to shore. There was no money for anything else, but the chips tasted fine. Who could ask for more? It was our first full day of married life.

Me man went quiet, then said, 'Is your family always going to treat you like they did yesterday?'

'I would have thought so, but since me Dad bought me a glass of lemonade last night, then in a few months' time, or maybe a few years, he'll probably take me back. After all, I made them lose face with other Travellers, by deserting them and being a renegade. I defied me parents, Terry, and that's hard to forgive.'

'Will I ever be a Traveller or Gypsy?' he asked.

This made me laugh. 'No, my love, you cannot become a Gypsy. You have to be born one. Why, do you want to be one?' I asked him.

'Yes, I want to be treated like your brothers are and take you to see your family sometimes. I want to be part of that life, Maggie.'

'Oh, my Terry, then I'll make you me Romani rye.'

'What's that then?'

'Well I'm a Romani and you're a rye. A rye is a rich man and you're rich for having me, so we'll put the two together and make you my Romani rye.' Then we laughed. 'I'm going to learn you all me language and how to get your living my way. I'm going to teach you how to handle and judge a horse – and you can learn me *your* ways as well. We'll combine both our knowledge and be strong and work hard together. Then we might be treated fairly. Yes, let's show me family we can do it.'

Chapter Fourteen

Our Life Together

WE HAD MANY BRIDGES TO CROSS, some smooth, some rough and tough, but when the going got hard we talked it through, usually after a good old row. Well I say 'row' – I had to row with meself because my mush would walk away from me when I kicked off on one. He was not one for a shouting match and hated it if we quarrelled.

It was a few years and two sons later before we really got to know each other. In that time we saw almost nothing of me family.

I was steeped in my culture and customs, which me man found hard to understand. He was an ex army man and set in his ways. Add to that, I found out something about him which shook me to me roots and worried the life out of me. I knew nothing of this part of his life for nigh on two years. We had had to leave the flat when I was expecting me first baby and we'd bought a trailer on a private site at Patchway in Bristol. (By now we had two children, one eighteen months old, the other a month old). One day we was sitting chatting in our old trailer when we caught sight of two mushes through the window. We had seen many debt collectors going to different trailers on the camp we lived on – you got to know how to pick them out – so we were watching to see who they would visit this time round when they veered off and headed towards *our* trailer.

What would they want with us? We owed no one any money.

'You don't owe any money anywhere, do you?' I asked Terry.

'No, I don't.'

Then me trailer door was nigh on ripped off its hinges and flung open.

'Terry Bendell?' the two big-built mushes asked.

'Yes?'

Before I could speak, they had me man gripped between them and were dragging him out the trailer.

'You got the wrong man,' I shouted. 'Let him go. Leave him be!'

One of them said, 'No, we got the right one.'

There they went frogmarching me man down the camp – and I could see they was getting rough in the process. So I grabbed me baby under me arm, stooped down to pick up me long, thin poker and told me older boy to follow me. Off we went after the mushes who by the time I caught up with them had bundled me man in the back of their car.

I was having none of this. My man was innocent. When I got near the car I noticed another mush sitting in the driver's seat with the window wound down. Up I creeps till I'm by the open window. I could dick the mush had his back to me – he was shouting at me man in the back. So I gently poke the poker into his ear...

'Now, mush,' I tells him, 'if you don't tell they two bastards to let me man out the car right now, this poker is going in this ear and out the other.' And I gave it a wiggle to prove me point.

The mush's head went rigid.

'Tell your wife to leave off,' one of the others told my Terry.

'She won't listen to me. I can't stop her. She means it and will do it,' he answered.

'Tell her to back off,' the driver said, so I gave him another wiggle for good measure, which made him start to get really worried.

'I shan't back off. Let me man out or this poker goes right through your head. You bastards – three to one. Well, not where I comes from. If you want a fair fight, I'll get you one any time you likes.'

'She means it. Me wife is a Gypsy and she means it,' said my Terry. 'She will kill you.'

Of course I meant it: me man was innocent – or so I thought just then.

'You got five days to come up with the forty quid you owe the betting office or else. We'll be back – and learn to control that wife of yours, she wants locking up. Let him out,' he told the two in the back. Which they duly did, but I kept me poker where it was.

'Forty quid?' I asked. 'What forty quid? What do my man owe you forty quid for?'

'Gambling!' he shouted at me, 'Gambling. That's what it's for – betting on dogs and horse races, Missus.'

'You better tell me we ain't in no debt for betting on races,' I told my Terry. He just hung his head and nodded. 'So we's forty pound in debt?'

'So they three said.' But I knew by the look on him it was true. Forty pounds was a small fortune in 1964.

'Well, you get back in that car because if they don't kill you, I will. He's all yours,' I said and grabbed me little boy and went back to me trailer. But they let him go, providing he came up with forty pounds we had no hope in hell of finding.

'I hope they mushes kills you stone dead,' I hollered at him. 'Forty bloody pounds – betting on fucking horses! I'll do for you. I promise if you comes near me, I'll cut your throat.'

He sat in the trailer while I went off me head. And as I cussed him – and meself for not knowing about it – he got a dejected look that I'd never seen on him afore.

'I'm a first-class dinalow,' I told meself. 'There he is, forty pounds in debt and I'm beginning to feel sorry for him.'

'You could borrow it off your Dad,' he said.

I could borrow it off me Dad. 'Oh yes,' I cried, 'he would love that, wouldn't he? For me to come crawling, begging a loan of forty pound because me man's been gambling – and they lot only just starting to visit me, and then only because I got two small chavvies. That's why they visits me – to make sure me chavvies is fed and well. I shan't – I can't show meself up, begging for money. No, I shan't ask me Dad for money. Go out and earn it.'

'How can I earn that sort of money in five days?'

'You spent it in five days, I'll bet.'

'No, Maggie, it's been building up a long time – five shillings here and there. I had a run of bad luck. All me mates do it – I picked it up in the army.'

'A run of bad luck? You must have had a hundred runs of bad luck. You bastard, Terry...'

'Help me, then. Help me and I promise I'll never put on another bet.'

'Let me think, afore I cuts that throat of yours,' I told him.

'Shall we have a cuppa?' he asks.

'We can't afford to eat or drink right now. How much money have we got right now?'

'About thirty shillings, but we ain't paid this week's rent and we need a new gas bottle.'

'That's put paid to that, then. I'm going to say this to you, Terry: if ever you bets again – I'm not threatening you, I'm making you a solemn promise – I promise you, if you bets again, I'll pick up me two chavvies and leave you ... and go where you'll never find me. Got that? I means it.'

'I know you means it. And I'll make *you* a solemn promise. I'll never bet again, not ever. And you'll never have to leave me.'

'Alright, I'll tell you what you have to do. You got to drive round and find out where the rubbish lorries tips their load – the dust carts as you call them. And don't come back afore you do. I want to know where the ash tips are.'

'What good will that do us?'

'Just do it. Find the tips.'

When he returned he had found two, but he was still puzzled as to why I wanted to know where the tips were.

'Right, while you been gone I've sorted out a few sack bags. Now drive us to those tips. It's after six so the places should be empty of workers.'

He's still thinking I've lost me marbles as he pulled up outside one of the dumps.

'You stay put and look after the babies. Shan't be long.'

Carrying me sacks, I climbed through the fence and was soon picking up bits of brass, copper, zinc and alloy, putting all me metals in separate sacks. Brass taps weigh well as do little old toy tractors and the like made of lead. All the time I was thinking, 'Me Dad would like this.'

Taking me time, before long I had me sacks ready for loading. I dragged them back to the fence one at a time then called my Terry to load them.

'What on earth have you got here?'

'Scrap metals,' I answered. 'And in the morning you'll drive me to the scrapyard. I knows where that is, I've been there with me Dad many times.'

On the morrow we pulled in the scrapyard.

'Me Dad Lenard Smith sent this in,' I says.

'Did he now?' smiled the mush, knowing me Dad's name.

'And he wants top prices... There'll be more tomorrow, he said to tell you.'

I done me weighing in and got more or less half the money we needed. I would go back to the tips again that night and get meself an even better load. Terry couldn't get over how I had earned all this money.

We got the money we needed in less than five days. And I made sure

Terry took me with him to pay it over. It really hurt me to give this money over for something I had had nothing to do with.

I hadn't shown Terry that way of earning money before. He liked the easiness of it and we continued to do it some evenings until we built up a small nest egg and got a decent car with it.

My Terry never broke his word to me. He gave up gambling – I know it was hard for him because he explained how he was addicted to it. He gave up his fags too, but he would still like a drink. That never really bothered me as I was brought up in a drinking family.

Terry had two passions in his life: one was coarse fishing and the other was to own his own horse. He would have to wait a few years for his horse but sometimes I would go to the river with him, to let the boys get the smell of the banks and water. Our Michael was only a toddler but Terry made him a little rod to hold in his hand.

We would take the boys to see Terry's parents but Terry's Dad's illness was catching up on him (we think he had cancer although it was not diagnosed as such) and the drugs he was taking made the poor mush do silly things. Michael was only eighteen months old and Terry's Dad tried to shave him, which worried me no end so I stopped taking my boys to their home. It was such a shame to see this very nice mush go downhill. Terry told me how, during the War, his father had been a radio operator on the planes bombing Germany and had been away from his family mostly all through the war. Not long after we lost his Dad which made us all very sad.

Terry kept on with his day job and some evenings we visited the tips. Me Dad come in one day and asked me how the scrap business was going.

'What scrap business?' I asked, smiling.

'The scrap you weighs in under my name to get more money for it.'

It was true, I used me Dad's name because the yard owner would offer different prices according to the customer. My Dad was a good customer so he got a better price, which I was getting for my family.

'A word of warning, my Maggie. Don't learn your gorgie mush too much of our ways.'

'Only enough to live,' I told him. There it was again – 'your gorgie mush' – he would never accept us two as a pair.

Then I had a visit from me Mam. She could drive now and she turned up driving me Dad's old lorry.

'Hello, Mam, it's kushti to dick yis. I spect you're dropping rag bills round here then?' They would call on me while dropping rag bills round the doors sometimes and I thought this was one of these times, but no, right away I was aware there was a specific reason for the visit.

'What's up, Mam, and where's me Dad then?' I asked.

'Oh yer Dad got things to do. I'm here to talk to you.'

'What about? What have I done now, Mam?'

'Well, for a start, my gal, you've put yourself in a tan [house]. Wasn't the trailer kushti enough for you now? What do yis want to live in a tan for?'

'Oh Mam, will you never understand?'

'No, my gal, if I lives to be hundred I'll never understand where I went wrong with you. I never brought yis up to live like this. Tis a gorgie you're turning into.'

'Oh I get it, Mam, you and me Dad been chatting about me. It's over the scrap business, ain't it, eh?'

'Yes, my gal, it is and you'm learning that gorgie mush to rokker.' She meant I was teaching my man to speak Romani.

'Mam, sit down and let me tell yis something' – for she looked as though she was up for a good set-to.

'I don't want to listen to you, my gal. I've come all these miles to put you right and put you right I will,' she told me.

'Alright, have your say. But if yis upsets me two babies I'll ask you to leave.' Me babies was playing out in the back garden and had not heard me Mam come in.

'My, you're getting uppity in your ways. "Ask me to leave".'

'Just have your say, Mam, then go and leave me be.'

'Right, this is how me and your Dad sees it. You got a gorgie mush, but that's not enough for you, is it, Maggie? You gotta go and learn the object all our ways. You got 'im scrap collecting, you got 'im rokkering our language. In fact you'm learning 'im all our crafts. Next he'll be a-hoss-dealin'.'

'Have yis finished, Mam?' I asked, me temper rising.

'No I have not, not by a longshot, I ain't.'

'Well, I'll have my say now, Mam. By God, you got a short memory, Mam. Remember when we was growing up and me Dad used to beat the shit out of yis, remember that, Mam?'

'That was our business and nothing to do with you,' she had the cheek to say.

Ignoring her, I carried on. I was determined to have my say now. 'Is that what yis two wanted for me? To have a man who would beat hell out of me? Is it, Mam?'

'I should have gived you a good hiding years ago,' she shouted.

'We all had good hidings, Mam. Every time me Dad knocked you down we chavvies felt it. Think on our Alfie. What was he, fourteen, when he first challenged me Dad out over you? He was just a boy, Mam, when he jumped out to me Dad.'

'Well that's in the past and nothing to do with the capers you're kicking up,' she said.

'Capers, Mam, capers? I married a man who looks after me and me two babies. He don't raise a hand to me – and God only knows I asks for it at times. And yes, Mam, I learns him to rokker and, while I'm on it, I'll warn yis now: I'll go on learning him to rokker the same as I do with me chavvies. And Mam, I swear to yis, I'll make me man as kushti a dealer as me Dad is afore I'm finished. Now go back and tell me Dad that.'

'I'll never speak to you again, my gal. And never is a long time.' She was crying now.

'Go on home, Mam. Just remember, you got your family and I got mine.'

'Yes, you got yer family, Maggie, and what a family it is. A bloody gorgie family. I hope yis proud of yourself.'

'Oh I'm proud, Mam. I'm very proud of what I got...' and *bang* went the door. Me Mam had left me nearly on me knees.

Well, it had to come. So much anger was bound to come out some time. But I had took the road I was meant to and now it was up to me and me man to make the best of that road. As me Mam drove away I swore to meself I would make the best of what I had. It was my doing, not theirs.

It's a shame so much hurt was caused by my love for a man. I fully understood me parents' feelings. I always recognised the hurt and despair I brought on my lot. Culture runs deep within our Romani families and cannot be breached.

That was not the end of me Mam and Dad's problems as far as their chavvies' marriages were concerned. I got blamed for all of it, but in turn I blamed *them* for buying that piece of land at Keel's Hill, because as one after another of me brothers and sisters grew up and took jobs in factories (which they could now that the family was no longer travelling) they met gorgie partners too. Not one of them married a Romani. It was maybe Sod's Law, as they say, but not one of these marriages worked. They all broke up except my own: mine was cemented hard from day one.

So you see, it's true what folks say, oil and water don't mix and we should never have given up travelling. To my mind that was the cause of me Mam and Dad's problems. We had loved our life on the roads and so had our parents, but in the end the life we were living pitted us against the Law: move on, get going, day in and day out we were being told to get out of it, move somewhere else – and the Law was strict in them days. To buy a small piece of land meant peace, but peace can come at a high price, such as the price me Dad paid by stopping in one place. Sad but true in our case.

Our son Michael with his Dad revisiting one of their many fishing haunts.

Life for me and my man continued to throw up new obstacles from time to time but we managed to climb over them. Our two boys was getting older and my Terry was ready to make fishermen out of them. Terry taught both our boys to fish from a young age. They loved it and I became a fishing widow, but I never minded because my three males was together enjoying themselves.

We brought our boys up in dwelling houses and gave them a full education – which meant a great deal to me: my own reading and writing was still very poor. I wanted our boys to follow my Terry, who was brilliant at the three R's, but I also wanted them to follow my culture closely too. We both wanted them to share our different backgrounds fully and I'm pleased to say both of them did.

My Terry became a dab hand at driving and breeding horses. It was second nature to him. He could hold his own with any hard-nosed dealer, something he learnt from me Dad, because after a few years the two of them became good friends. Terry was still a gorgie in their midst – he was never accepted as one of us, but I made sure he got treated fairly. He was *my* man and I looked out for him. He got to know my Romani language as well as I did myself; he embraced my culture and lived a big part of his life by it, as I did his. When we first got married he would sometimes say, 'I'll never get the hang of all this,' and I would coax him along: 'Yes you will, my love.' And he did.

Me family made it up with me. I knew they would. Me Dad could never stay bad friends with me for long; he always had to see and chat to his Maggie. But me Mam and me had a sort of distance between us which lasted her lifetime. Oh she loved me in her own way, but I was the instigator of her beloved family losing some of her old culture and customs she held so dearly to her heart and that was not to be forgiven too lightly. Not that I ever lost the true Romani my parents had bred in to me. I had too many generations of our culture in me to lose sight of it, as most of my community have. As the old Gypsy saying goes, 'Yis can't git from yer rear.' It means you shouldn't try to shake off your roots and make out you're something you're not.

In the early years Terry's dear mother would be mesmerised by me, when she and his Dad came to visit.

'Why on earth do you need so many buckets and bowls?' she would ask.

'One for washing up, one for washing me vegetables, one for soaking me teacloths and tablecloths in. A bucket for me nappies, a bucket to wash me floor and a bowl to wash our hands and faces in.'

'But why?' she would ask. 'I only use one...'

'Then you're a very dirty woman,' I once told her. 'I would *never* wash in the bowl I use for food.'

'And you're a silly girl,' she told me.

Her home was spotless, but I still believed her to be dirty because she used the same bowl for everything. And I made excuses not to have anything to eat or drink off her. Then on one visit I saw her let her big juckle drink out her cup: that put the lid on the can as far as I was concerned – for people to know that juckles lick all parts of their bodies and then let them feed off their plates and drink out their cups. To us Romanies that is considered very dirty indeed.

So you see, me man had a lot to put up with, God love him. He encouraged me to be just me – the gal he married. Over the years we became as one. We relied on each other and had a deep love affair that never ended. It took death to part us. But the love lives on. If my man had lived another six days we would have reached our fiftieth wedding anniversary.

I lost him to a sarcoma-type cancer aged seventy one. He bore his illness with dignity and never moaned. He accepted he had it, but I could not accept that I was to lose the mainstay of me life – my friend, my lover, my husband and my life's pal. Of course we tried the radiation treatment but it only worked for a little while.

When we were told we only had a few months left, we sat and cried and talked about it. We would have one last Christmas together then I would be on me own. No, my dearest lover, I told him, if you go I go.

Our problems had started when he was sixty-five. He had been in full employment since he was fourteen, apart from two years doing his National Service. He had enjoyed that and was about to sign on again for more of the same when he met me. But instead he had held some kushti jobs, such as being a manager in the local stone quarry. His real trade was as a pipe fitter. He held this job for many years, but over the years he had also worked for himself selling nuts and bolts and stuff to the engineering trade and for his last job he held a taxi-driving licence and had his own mini bus. He would work all hours of the day and night. Yes, he was a hard worker. On weekends or at horse fairs he would wheel and deal as well.

Then at sixty-five he retired. A month later he had a stroke. He woke up in the middle of it one morning. Afterwards, we sat down and talked about it and I promised him we would beat this stroke, which over time we did. He got well again, but the stroke left him with a little lump on the front of his left leg. Over time it grew bigger and the doctors was confused as to what it was. He was misdiagnosed for four and a half years. In the end it was diagnosed coincidentally when he was sent for a heart bypass test: a heart doctor told him he had a malignant sarcoma – not heart problems.

A few days later the diagnosis was confirmed by a cancer specialist in Bristol who thought treatment might help. By now the lump had grown to the size of a football. The hospital staff couldn't get over the size of the tumour and I could read between the lines as they talked to us – I knew I was on borrowed time with my man.

He had a few sessions of radiation. The tumour on his leg went down, but others grew like a field of mushrooms. They came out of every part of his body, including three on his head, but still he carried on as normally as his illness would allow, even doing a few deals here and there.

It's part of my culture at such times to go back to happy places you have been to in the past. We went back to the layby where my Terry proposed marriage to me – we had a laugh because we had both aged over the years.

Not long after that me mind went into overdrive. After all these years, he would have no choice but to leave me. Selfish though it may seem, I made up me mind that, if possible, I would go with him.

Our last visit to the hospital was on the 7th October 2010. That was the day the specialist told us to 'go home and put your life in order, you have only a few months.'

As I drove home from Bristol Terry said to me, 'You do know this will be me last Christmas, don't you?'

'And it will be mine too.'

I had made up me mind over the previous few miles that when I hit Wells Hill I would end it for both of us...

'This will be our last ride together,' I told the love of me life.

'Will it, my old gal?'

'Yes,' I said as I picked up speed, making sure no one was driving in front or behind me. 'We're going right through that wall ahead,' I told him, 'just you and me together. I love you, my Terry, I'm coming with you.'

'Just think of our boys and what that would do to them,' he said. He never told me to slow down, just to think of the boys.

I slowed down, but I said again, 'I want to come with you.'

'You can't, my old gal – we can't do that to the boys.'

So we went on together, still living our life. Until towards the end of November, when I took ill and ended up in hospital. I had caught meself a chest infection and I went to our doctor and begged him to give me drugs to make me well quickly as my husband was very ill and needed me to help him. I was given two flu injections and antibiotics to take. The next day I felt truly bodily ill and went back to the doctor, who gave me a bottle of cough mixture. By now I had a water infection as well as the chest infection and within days I was shaking and shivering like a wet dog. I was so cold my Terry would put me in a hot bath to warm me up. Terry sent for the doctor again and he gave me yet more antibiotics and told my man I would be fine. The next day my sister Emily visited me and did not recognise me. I had lost so much weight, it was falling off me. My Terry was in tears and so they rang 999 and I was taken away on the blue light to hospital.

It turned out I was very ill indeed. I had septicaemia from the flu injections. I felt I was mullering (dying). I lost days in that hospital, not knowing where I was. Then the drugs kicked in and I started to feel better, but nearly a fortnight had passed and as Terry visited me I saw a big change in my man. He pined so much for me. Each day our son brought him in to visit me, but I could see that, each day, he was falling a little further behind in the race. I begged the doctors to let me home – 'You're too ill to go home,' I was told.

'Then, Doctor, when it's visiting time, please just walk through the ward and take a look at my man. Then you'll see why I have to get home.'

God bless that doctor, he did as I asked and packed me off home the next morning, loaded down with antibiotics and other medicine. He understood that my man's need outweighed my own.

My Terry fed me and looked after me like a newborn baby. We were both in a mess. I asked the Good Lord to take us both and end me misery. Our daughter-in-law cooked us meals and our two boys was here all the time, but all we two wanted was each other – holding hands, giving each other cuddles.

With my love's care each day I got a little better, but I had to get me hair cut short as I couldn't manage it.

'You looks nice,' he said when I got back from the hairdressers.

'Yeah, I dicks like a mush with short back and sides.'

We kept going till Christmas. Our two boys came and ate Christmas dinner with us – for the first time in over twenty years. They gave up their family day to spend it with us, all of us knowing but not saying, this is our final Christmas together.

My love took another stroke on a Sunday afternoon. It was a blessing for my Terry, but oh so very hard for me. He went into hospital but I got him home by the next night. He lived five more days with me and the boys sitting and holding him before he slipped peacefully away on 4th March 2011. St Margaret's Hospice were wonderful – they got my Terry home and he knew he was in his own bedroom. I have still the bedding he died in on me bed: the sheets, unwashed, are folded up and placed under the pillows he laid his dear head on. I sleep each night on the spot where he died. In my mind we are still together as long as I sleep with that bedding. It comforts me in me own way.

When Terry was getting so poorly, I got a little container and started to save up me nail cuttings. I did this right up till he died. Often he would ask me why I was doing this daft thing, but I just told him it was something I had to do. The nail clippings I saved up were put in a little box and placed in his right hand before he was laid to rest – so a part of me is still in his grasp even now.

So that was my mixed marriage. True love brought us along that long, rough road. Nothing could part us but death.

The day I buried me man, I buried me heart in the deep cool earth.

Mixed marriages can work – but at a cost. The price can be high, I know that first hand. Back in the days when I brought my man into the Gypsy community, it was not the done thing. It was seen more as a crime. It meant an outsider would learn our ways, which had been so closely, not to say jealously, guarded for hundreds of years. After all, the older generations had paid dearly because of who they were, and the message, 'Never trust a gorgie', had been passed down and down the generations.

You may wonder why I never turned my back on me family, when they treated me and my man so badly. It was because I knew I had broken our rules – it was me who caused our family to lose face in front of other Travellers, me who caused me Mam and Dad to get sly, deep remarks thrown at them – 'What were you thinking of, Lenard, letting your gal have a gorgie mush?'

What I did wasn't unknown, it had happened before, but each family where it happened paid the price of one of their own running off with a gorgie. The price I paid was to lose the respect of me Mam at the age of twenty. She never forgave me or fully accepted my man – she was quite open about it and would run him down in front of me face. She never let me forget what I had done. But I forgave her. I had asked for

My brother Richard.

what I got; I had let them down according to our culture and tradition, I admit it.

As for me Dad, yes, I think I gained his forgiveness. We had a close relationship and worked well together: I loved me Dad dearly.

But I can't say he ever forgot that my Terry was not of our blood. The first few years he rubbed it in like salt in a wound. It would be

'Your gorgie this', 'Your gorgie that' – my man could do no right. But as the years passed, he mellowed and they became a right pair of horse dealers, they would even deal with each other. My Terry would never let me Dad get the best of him on a deal: if he wanted to do a deal with me Dad, even after he'd been dealing for many years, I would judge the gry and tell him its true worth, and that's how my man would hold his own on a deal with me Dad. Dad would say to me, 'Your Terry's a hard mush to deal with,' which I took as a huge compliment: my man had nothing more to prove.

Out of me two older brothers, Robert never really gave way, even though he and Terry got on together. But there was always an undercurrent ready to be opened up. Our Alfie, yes, he liked my Terry well enough, but underneath I always felt he was jealous simply because of how close Alfie and I had been before I got married – but he never stopped being protective of me.

My sisters Emily and Holly in their own way took to and loved my old boy. Emily still says, 'Your Terry was the gentleman of our family,' and she's right, he was always a gentleman.

As for the youngest two, Richard and Mo, they was very young and took no notice of what he was or wasn't. They accepted him and to them he was just 'our Terry'.

My Terry and me built our own family tree between us and that tree is so strong a tornado couldn't knock it down. We gave our two boys both sets of values – we gave them all the love we had so that they know how to give it and to pass it on to their families, which is so important for future generations. Values and principles are a must to keep a family strong. I know this because my own family had them, I grew up with them.

Identity is also very important. In a way I have lived two lives – my own traditional Gypsy way and the gorgie way, especially when it came to dwellings. But I admit I never settled down to life in dwellings: I just couldn't come to terms with being shut in a house. Give me a wagon or

*Me Mam and Dad with their granddaughter Bonnie on the land where I now live.
These were the days me Dad was so happy with his mares and foals.*

trailer any day of the week, let me live where I can smell the hedgerows
and hear the first song of the birds as the dawn breaks above me. I need
to smell the wood smoke as the breeze gently spreads it across the fields.
It's all there embedded in my blood. Us Romani Gypsies have a passion
for nature and we need to be close to it. We see the deep beauty of the
plants and animals – it's a big part of our daily lives.

Terry and I were lucky to have our own private site and to own a couple
of acres of land which had belonged to me Dad, family land. I still live
there to this day and hopefully will die there too.

We kept our grys in the paddock and lived close by them. Thick
hedges on all sides gave us our privacy. Each morning we were greeted

by the juckles and grys – in dry weather our first cuppa was drunk out in the yard while chatting to our animals. We walked the paddock with them at our heels and would stop by Old Storm's grave, under the big oak tree. Storm was me Dad's old driving mare – we had her buried on the land she had spent many of her years on. Her grave is fenced in but the squirrels still manage to bury their walnuts and hazelnuts on her grave. Every few years we had to move and replant the nut bushes and young walnut trees this produced, otherwise we would have ended up living in a copse. That would have been lovely, but the grass was more important, to feed the grys.

We have a fox that cuts across the paddock in search of food and we still get the deer who used to share our grys' hay in winter – they come in the snow looking for a feed, but there's no hay kept here now. It's kushti to watch them out the window, walking about unafraid of us. We never hounded them, it was nice to see them all feeding together.

Sometimes, when me feet got itchy for the open road, I would ask my man to hitch up one of our wagons so we could wander off for a few weeks, taking to the back roads and lanes.

'Let's do it, my love, just me you and the wagon and gry. I will show you a part of my life that is free. We'll be as free as the birds,' I would tell him.

But he wouldn't. This is one of the only things he could not do for me. His reasons was sound and true. He'd say, 'I couldn't live like you, on the road, my Maggie,' and deep down I knew he couldn't.

He wanted to take his bath and toilet along with him; it was the personal things he couldn't cope with. And I respected that – that was part of who he was, so, alas, we never travelled in a horse-drawn wagon together, which would have made me life complete because I never gave up my dream of returning to the road. Yes, we travelled in trailers and would pull on campsites or private sites to be able to use their showers and toilets, but if you're a true Gypsy, life is better riding behind a good, steady piebald gry with a creaking wagon with smoke coming out the chimney pipe.

How I would have loved to take him back to some of our old stopping places, light a yog and cook him a meal from an old black pot, then sit round the embers and exchange tales of our different lives. His army days and my hawking times, knocking on house-dwellers' doors. Climb up in our wagon to spend a cosy night under the stars, with rain beating down on our canvas roof. Oh that sharing of my old life with my man would have been heaven for me. We could have relived the old days – my old days – with the wind blowing our hair and smoke in our yocks.

Up round the old Emborough Pond lanes would have been sheer bliss, me Dad's country, where the ghosts of long-gone Gypsies could have shared our yog once again, for old times' sake.

It's dreams, just dreams, after all these years.

But what is not just dreams is the fact that my man supported and encouraged me to be the activist I became. Terry was proud of the work I do and encouraged me all the way. I have him to thank for making me the person I am today and for the help it enabled me to give to my community.

Chapter Fifteen

My Romani Rye's Funeral

I BURIED MY MAN in the little cemetery in Street which is tucked away on a by-lane. It's off the beaten track and close to our private site, so if I needed to I could walk to it. But in doing so I made one of the biggest mistakes of me life, because had I been in me right mind I could have had my love buried in our own horse paddock, where I could have had a cuppa and a fag with him any time I liked, which would have been often.

The days between Terry's passing and the funeral were like a bad dream. I think me mind went elsewhere. During our custom of sitting up, the days ran into each other. Sitting up is our custom when family and friends spends their days and nights with the bereaved family – from the time of the death until the funeral. I had the best of the best attend me: gals turned up to keep the kettle on the boil to make tea, my friends and relatives showed their true colours and stayed by me day and night, bringing with them tea, sugar and milk to keep us all going. Some wonderful people played their part and sat up with me and our

The horse-drawn carriage for my Terry's funeral.

two sons day and night. We had very few minutes alone, which is part of our culture. Even though my man was not Romani, everyone treated his sitting-up period as if he was one of them – the barriers was down: he was Maggie's man and that was good enough for one and all.

During our trips to the hospital for his cancer treatment, my Terry had learnt a song I used to play in the car as we travelled up and down to Bristol: 'You're my Best Friend' by Don Williams. He would ask me to play the CD and we would sing every word to each other, so when I wrote a piece to have read in church during his service, I also had our song played. We all sang along as best we could and I could hear my Terry singing it with us in my ear. It broke me heart all over again.

Then there were the Boys. These were a pair of majestic black Friesian horses owned by Jimmy Searle from Oakhanger in Hampshire.

I had helped Jimmy and his wife with their planning application and my Terry used to come up to Jimmy's place with me. Jimmy would

Jimmy Searle with the Boys, down from Hampshire on the morning of the funeral.

harness the Boys up to a carriage and take my Terry and me all over the common land, which Terry so enjoyed. He would talk about these two fantastic grys all the way home. My man became very fond of the Boys and when I was planning his funeral I rang Jimmy to ask for the Boys to carry my man one last time. These two grys were to be my special last gift to my man from me: he rode behind them in life and he would ride behind them on his last journey.

Terry was a very dignified man in life and I wanted a dignified funeral for him. I hope I achieved that much. It was a mixed funeral – my Romanies and his gorgies – all came and paid him their respects.

His black headstone, which I designed for him, is now in place. It shows three fishing rods on the top of his stone bearing the names of Michael, Terry and Jason, my three fishermen, and a lovely photo of my man smiling. And standing proud at the foot of the stone is a large carving of my Terry holding the halter of his favourite bay mare. These two carvings was made out in India because they have the hardest

My dear Terry's headstone.

The other side of the headstone.

granite in that country. They are carved in white granite. That was my gift to my man for his love of horses. On the back of the headstone there is an etching of our Reading wagon with the words 'Our Forgotten Years'. It was Terry who gave me the title of my first book. Then the words of 'You're my Best Friend', a little altered to suit us both, topped off with our one and only honeymoon picture.

Of course I've left room to add my own death date.

He never looked down at my lot but had the gift to take each of them on their own merit. All of which shows what kind of man he was. His love of horses grew over the years and each horse that passed through his hands had a grand life, being owned by him. We laughed many times over one particular horse he looked after for a close friend of ours. The owner of that horse made holly wreaths at Christmas and, as it's such a busy time, he asked my Terry to have his gry for a few weeks. The horse came to us and settled in well; each morning at six my man would get the horses out of the paddock, having put their feed out in the stables ready for them – each gry had its own stable. In they would run – our friend's gry only took a couple of days to work out which stable was hers and soon got into the routine of feeds at six in the morning and five at night afore being let out to graze. That was Terry's way of doing things. The day came when our friend took his gry back home to her own stable – only to come back a few days later, laughing, as he told my Terry, 'You've ruined me mare.'

'How come?' asked me man.

'Because ever since I got her back, she kicks her stable door and whickers at peep of daylight and fetches me out me bed. I can't sleep, man, she gives me no peace till I gets up and feeds her. You ruined her.' Unlike my man, he was not an early riser. He took it all in good spirit, but he never let my Terry look after his mare the next year. It became a long-standing joke between them.

Then came the sad day when Terry realised he could not care for his grys as he used to. He was becoming too ill and weak.

'Maggie, I got to get rid of me grys,' he said with tears in his yocks.

I had known this was coming because I would stand and watch how he struggled to look after them. It hurt me to see a gentle nudge from one of his grys, a nudge of love, nearly knock him off his feet. But the decision had to come from him – there was no way I could tell him he was getting too weak to handle his beloved grys.

'What have you got in mind?' I asked him.

'I'm going to ring Nelson Turner.'

Nelson was a close friend and Terry knew how well he cared for his own grys, so it was decided that Nelson would take and sell our grys – all five of them.

'Are you sure you wants to do this?' I asked Terry.

'Maggie, look at me. I've looked after them till I know I can't cope any more – they five grys deserve somebody younger and fitter. I haven't been able to drive them in months either. No, it's best they go.'

The phone call was a painful one for Terry to make. He couldn't bring himself to tell Nelson what he wanted to see him for, but Nelson agreed to come down the next day.

True to his word, Nelson came down from Blandford, Dorset, the next day and I could see the stress on my old Terry's face.

'What's up, Terry?' asked Nelson while we all had a cuppa.

'I got a job for you.' Those were my Terry's favourite words.

'Oh and what's that then?'

'Fetch your lorry down, pick up they five horses and sell them to good homes. I can trust you to make sure that they gets proper good homes, can't I, Nelson?'

'Yes, you can, but I never thought to hear you say it. Are you sure, Terry?'

I caught Nelson's eye and he understood. 'Of course I shan't let you down,' he said. 'They'll go to good homes. I might keep a couple meself

*My Terry with his foal Sunny. They were together for years and Sunny
would drive my man to the pub.*

– how's that then?'

My Terry could say no more – it was done.

The horses went the following day, a day too painful to write down.
It was a terrible wrench for Terry to part with his beloved grys and he
pined for them there after. Each time a horse-dealer called in, it was
touch and go. He still wanted to have a gry and I would read his
thoughts in his face: 'I might have meself a deal here in a minute.' It
would not have surprised me.

He kept an album of photos of most all the grys he ever owned and
he remembered all their names off by heart. Over the years he had
owned hundreds – and bred some good ones into the bargain.

When I married my Terry I gave up very little of me old life. I didn't
have to because he embraced my life: he became a Gypsy mush in
everything bar blood and we had a kushti full life. That's why I'm

My Terry with his favourite dog 'The Whinger'.

struggling to go on without him. People say to me, 'But, Maggie, you got all them memories.' What people don't realise is, yes, memories is lovely but by God they hurt.

Each day, though, I see Terry's likeness in my son Jason's face – and he's just like his Dad for wheeling and dealing. Our other son, Mike, is also one not to pass up a deal, so my man will live on through these two.

God bless you, my Terry, for being you.

Chapter Sixteen

Memories of Happier Times

ME DAD WAS SITTING NEXT TO ME driving our old gry Patchie as the wagon slowly made its way along the quiet road. With me long skinny legs hanging over the foreboard of our wagon, I was in me element, as happy as I could be. We slowed up to pull in and wait for me Mam and our Alfie to catch up with us after they had hawked the last village we had passed through – Ilchester near Yeovil. It was that little mush's turn to help me Mam today. They were calling with bunches of sweet-smelling primroses which we had picked the afternoon before while we were pulled in on the wild hills near Street. Everywhere you walked you stepped on the flowers, which grew so thickly it was like a huge carpet.

As the basket full of flowers had been placed on the bunk bed as we travelled, the perfume still lingered in our wagon now. Having pulled in, me and me Dad and little Jess and our Robert set about making our camp. We three chavvies fetched wood while me Dad unhitched his gry from the wagon. Then he would light the yog while we fetched drinking water then went back to fetch more for the two grys to drink. Dad made sure they cooled down afore they filled up on water as they could ketch their death of a chill if they drank cold water while they was still too hot.

For the rest of the spring and summer we would be living in a perfumed world of wild flowers and bushes, each day a new stopping place or a field to work in and nature at its best. As a youngster, who could ask for more?

Me Dad called over to me, 'Maggie, fill yer Mam's pots and stick 'em near the yog, then peel the stralks [potatoes] ready for when they two gets back.'

Because they had parted up me and our Alfie it was peaceful, but it was a sure thing we would get to fighting again on his return, because with his pretty face housewives were apt to give him little treats which he liked to keep to himself – and which I always wanted a share of. So it would come to blows between us. But for now it was grand – just the three of us and me Dad working side by side.

Then, when there was no sign of Alfie and me Mam, Dad told us to stay by the wagon; he would ride one of our mares back to meet the other two. He was worried someone might have moved the clumps of grass he had left on the crossroads to show me Mam which way we had gone – which sometimes happened. Then she would walk on in the wrong direction and be upset for days, not to mention her sore feet. Locals in the villages we travelled through regular had got to know some of our habits. They knew about the clumps of grass and would move them as a joke, but it was no joke if one of us took a wrong turn. Hence the men would go out seeking their women and chavvies after a certain period of time had gone by.

So it was a relief to see our little group walking towards us from the direction of the village. Just as our ancestors had, we tried to pull in where we were less noticeable, less visible to the local community. If a little-used lane was handy, the wagons would be backed up in it, right off the highway. Then the hawkers would be guided back by the smell of wood smoke. It was often useless for them to try to follow the wheel-rim tracks because there was others using horses and carts on these roads: coalmen, bakers, milkmen and of course the farmers with their horses pulling farm machinery.

We sat round the yog eating our much-needed meal while me Mam and Dad discussed where to head for, to avoid bumping into too many other Travellers like ourselves. More Travellers meant more hawkers in the same area, and according to their talk, we was doing nicely on our own and earning a fair living.

'Let's try our luck around Blandford for a change,' said me Dad.

'Fine by me, my Len, we ain't been that way in ages.'

So we took the winding road through Yeovil, then up into the hills to an area that had wide grass verges and little bits of common land that we could pull on. Me Dad knew them all; he also knew where we would likely come across the Dorset Travellers with whom we would share a yog for a few days before moving on. We travelled through Sherborne and Sturminster Newton to Blandford and then north to common land at Shaftesbury, finally heading back across to Gillingham and out onto the Wincanton road towards our own area.

While me Dad made clothes pegs, me and me Mam called the doors to hawk them off, earning money as we travelled from village to village. These were good days – long days when our little family was just that, a family, with me Dad kept out of the kitchermas and off the brown ale. Deep down, me Mam was keeping him away from his brothers, whom she thought led him astray. When they were all together, where one went the rest would follow – and hard-earned shillings would disappear out of pockets and down their long necks.

Oh, she was cute, me Mam, and persuaded me Dad that we should keep travelling on our own.

'How much have we earned and saved?' he would ask.

'Oh, not a lot,' she'd answer, telling him of only a portion of what she had tucked in her skirts, for vonger and me Dad were soon parted. 'Why is you asking?'

'Because I spotted a little tit [horse] back yonder I might be able to deal for.'

'I never dicked no nice little tit, my Len.'

'That's cuz you weren't looking, my Vie. Kin we go back for a second look?' he pleaded.

'You can dick all yis wants, my Len, and want will be your master. We ain't got vonger enough for no grys.'

'What? I must have made hundreds of dozens of pegs these last few weeks – and you sold 'em all. And we ain't got the price of a gry?'

'So you have, my Len, but at the same time you have ate well and smoked like a chimney. I got maybe thirty shillings saved up' – all the time having fifty shillings tucked away. Yes, she was cute, me Mam, and we loved her for it.

Back in our own country, as me Dad used to say, we pulled in Frome Lanes with the Frome Lane gang – very old-fashioned Travellers, the old Hughes and Coopers. I took to the little town of Frome with its steep, winding streets – it held many surprises round its narrow bends and it's a fair pretty place to hawk and shop. Having got news of his family, me Dad wanted to meet up with them, so we said our farewells and headed for Radstock, pulling in at Round Hill between Peasedown St John and Radstock.

This was a kushti place to pull in off the highway. It was possible to walk on down the lane into the centre of Radstock and in the opposite direction lay Peasedown and me Dad's family. It was also a coal-mining area with rows upon rows of miners' cottages in every village – little did we dream as we played in those lanes, watching the miners make their way to and from work, that one day me brother Alfie would join them and work deep underground, so he could earn vonger to buy a motorbike and clothes. He loved clothes and looking smart and was prepared to go underground and dig out coal to buy such things.

What with his love of nature and daylight and of running free, it was a real shock to all of us when he come back to Keel's Hill (a piece of ground me Dad bought for us to stop on years later) and told us proudly, 'I'm a coal miner.' Now, as we played and fought each other, I would never have been able to imagine me brother being like a mole under the ground. It's a good job we can't see into the future.

Stopping on Round Hill gave us chavvies a bit more freedom to roam and wander the fields, because there were always me Dad's brothers and their families visiting us, spending hours sitting round our yog, chatting and laughing. We took the opportunity to escape with their chavvies and a gang of us would wander away for hours of fun, always returning with an armful of wood for the yog, to make good our claim that we had not been idle.

Then me Dad would brag to his brothers, 'Just dick at me kushti chavvies – *my* lot don't fergit to work.'

It felt good to hear ourselves bragged up, instead of being threatened with a good hiding for bickering, which me and our Alfie did often. We were too much alike for our own good.

The gavvers was usually quite kushti when we stopped here. They knew all of us by name. They also knew our habit of travelling back to check out the old couple living down Prince Lane, so would stop for a chat and leave us be, knowing we would soon move on. Oh, if only all the gavvers had treated us this way, life would have been so much better, but it's a burden we had to bear, being moved on more or less daily, with a few insults thrown in for good measure. If they had only taken the time to understand that we meant no harm to anyone and that our aim was to work and live a peaceful life. But the distrust was born many hundreds of years earlier and stuck fast within their minds. We had no choice but to live with it.

Me Dad took us chavvies down the Lane a few times when he visited his parents. We got hugs and kisses from our dear Grandad, but we gave the old Granny a wide berth. She did not love us one bit, because she had never taken to our Mam (who never set foot in the Lane if she could help it). Me Mam, being a little spitfire, would at times lay into our Granny when the old woman was at her worst – and that could be often. For no good reason the old Granny would start.

'Just look at you, then,' she would shout at me Mam. 'Whatever did me son see in the likes of you? You can't even get your own living.'

'Get me living?' answered me Mam. 'Old woman, I can out-call you any day of the week. I can sell me pegs quicker than you any time, anywhere.'

'Yis ought to be back in Devonshire where yis belongs, with your gorgie family,' shouted the old Granny. (She never believed me Mam was a Traveller till me little brother Jessie got killed in 1950 and all me Mam's family travelled up for the funeral.)

'No, it's you who ought to go to Devonshire and meet some real proper Travellers, you bloody old cow,' answered me Mam.

Oh doughty, that done it.

'And we ain't proper Travellers?' me Dad said.

And so the old Granny had done it again and got me Mam and Dad at it, which was all she wanted. She really was a nasty old woman and although it was wrong we chavvies couldn't stand the sight of her at any price. That's the reason we tried to stay away from the Prince Lane or only go there when she and Grandad was off travelling.

Once me Dad had made sure all was well with his Mum and Dad, we shifted on. We had missed the pea-picking season this year, but as we had travelled about on our own, we had done well pocket-wise. Jim and May were coming with us – we were off on the long journey to the hop country.

We were pulled out and were waiting to see Jim's wagon appear down the main tober, or to hear the sound of his gry's shoes hitting the tarmac as it pulled its heavy load.

'Here they comes,' shouted our Robert, 'here they comes.'

We were full of excitement because we would have Jimmy, Lilea, Sibby and little Checkers to play with for the next few months. They were Jim and Aunt May's chavvies. And I was most pleased of all, because I had me Uncle Jim travelling along with us. I dearly loved me Uncle Jim, he being me favourite out of all me Dad's relations. Although me Dad and his brothers fell out from time to time, there was never a miss (a bad word) between Jim and me Dad. He was long and thin, just like me Dad, and wore the same kind of trilby staadi (hat). He was the most peaceful man, very kind and always skint – or nearly always. But travelling with this wonderful couple completed my happiness and me Mam's for she and Aunt May got on like a house on fire as well.

So it was a happy little band that headed for Bristol and the A38, which would lead us up to Ledbury in Herefordshire and the hop gardens.

We were in no hurry and had left nice and early, leaving plenty of time to travel the distance, so as not to rush our grys on their long pull. It was kushti because me and Lilea went out hawking with me Mam and May. Most days we would be dropped off at the start of a village, with dozens of wooden flowers of all colours, beautiful wooden chrysanthemums whittled from elder sticks. The hawking baskets glowed with colour, which helped to sell our craftwork, made by our men folk.

These flowers cost us nothing to make, only the time it took to make them. It was the same with the clothes pegs and willow baskets: all the materials we needed grew in the woods and hedgerows and land owners never minded us thinning out thick hedges. It was all part of life in the countryside.

As young chavvies we enjoyed going out hawking and getting first chance at any togs or shoes which our mams begged off the house-dwelling wives. And sometimes they would swap coupons out of their ration books for things we really needed – a bit of tea and sugar were the main things we bartered for. Clothing coupons meant very little to us, but tea and sugar did.

The wooden flowers went well. Aunt May had begged a kushti bundle of chavvies' togs – too small to fit me and Lilea, so we played up when we were asked to help carry them the few miles back to the wagons. May had split them up into four bundles so we could all carry a share. We tied them into bundles like this because our women never liked to put other people's clothes (no matter how clean) in the hawking baskets in which they carried their shopping. To us that would be dirty. This is one of the reasons we used prams for going out hawking, if we were ever offered one by some kind lady. A pram was a very welcome gift: everything would get shoved in and the hawking basket put on the top. It saved struggling to carry things which got heavier the further we had to walk. Make no mistake, we did a great deal of walking back then.

On this particular day Mam and May had begged a few cabbages and managed to buy a couple of hocks of bacon, so our meal tonight would be a tasty one of boiled bacon, taters and cabbage all cooked in the one pot, topped off with plenty of pepper and a pinch of salt. The fat out the bacon and the meat that falls off the bones puts so much flavour into the meal. If you have never tried this, then please do. It's so tasty and filling: this is old-fashioned Romani cooking.

Travelling along with May and Jim, it was as though our family had grown. Having Jimmy and Lilea to play with was like having extra brothers and sisters; we would have great fun just fetching wood and water or minding the grys (when the grys were let loose to give them some freedom, we chavvies would be sent up the road to turn them back if they tried to slip past us, but they would be off their plug chains for a couple of hours and had the freedom to graze near the wagons). On other occasions we would be taught to pick the right plants for potions to treat a cut or bruise or an illness one of our grys might have. We were never allowed to make these potions but were made to watch closely how it was done. I suppose you could call it an art: too little of this or too much of that could knock a gry off its feet. It was the same when our mams taught us the art of making cough medicine and rubs – everything that went into these things was judged by a keen yock. It may not have tasted good but it always worked for us.

Yes, it was kushti in many ways to be travelling with Jim and May. One advantage was that Jim was not so keen to run to the nearest kitcherma and encourage me Dad to get skirmish – not like some of Dad's other brothers who, with a nod and a wink, would disappear in a flash down to the village kitcherma and come rolling back skint but happy.

As we travelled and hawked, cooked and washed, the miles slipped by and each day brought us closer to the hop gardens. Sometimes we caught up with other families, stayed to chat and have a cuppa, then went on our way. Our lot were determined to travel on their own because the gavvers was on to us to keep on the move and the bigger the group travelling together the more abuse we got. It was hate on both sides: the gavvers hated us and we hated them. It's horrible not to be liked or trusted when all you want to do is lead a peaceful life and earn a bit of a living as you go about your daily life and bring up your family.

Chapter Seventeen

In the Hop Gardens Once Again

AFTER A SLOW, LEISURELY JOURNEY we reached the farm in the Hereford area where we would be picking hops. Jim and me Dad left us on the roadside while they went to book us in. We had picked hops here many times so the men were known to the farmer and soon we were pulling through the gate of the familiar field. First of all we stopped to pick out the spot we wanted.

'How's about if we takes that corner?' said Jim. 'If we pulls across it, we could light our yog right in the corner and get out of sight of the rest of the field. And,' he added, 'it will give us a bit of shelter from the weather.'

'Kushti, my brother,' answered me Dad, 'kushti.'

So we pulled both wagons across the corner and lit up a yog from the huge pile of wood the farmer had dropped off ready for his pickers to use. Then we fetched cans of water from the tap by the gate.

Farmers did not provide toilets in those days, so for years things had been mapped out by the Romanies. It was taken for granted that the woods behind the field were for the use of women and children only, the men would walk or drive off to find their own private place. God help any male that was caught near the women's wood. This was a very strict custom, respected by one and all.

As we settled in the field which would be our stopping place for the next few weeks, we knew peace for the first time in months. No gavver could move us out and on from here. While our first meal was simmering in the black pots the talk turned to shopping. The farmer had offered to loan the men his cart to take May and me Mam shopping, it being a bit too far to walk. So after our meal we older ones would be left in charge of the younger ones while the four grown-ups went into the town of Ledbury.

'I want to get meself a kushti side of bacon which should last us a couple of weeks,' said me Mam to May.

'And I gins just the right butcher to get it from,' laughed May.

'Not that old smoky bacon,' said Jim, 'I can't stick the taste of that rubbish.'

'Beggars can't be choosers,' teased me Mam, knowing full well they never bought the smoked sides of bacon.

Some families loved the smoky taste and others preferred the 'white' bacon, as they called it. The sides of bacon was bound up in muslin so could be kept on the tailrack of the wagon and slices cut off when needed. Many different meals could be made with bacon and our lot knew them all.

After they had gone, we were left on the field to keep the yog going and look out for the younger chavvies. We had been warned not to leave the wagons so we sat happily chatting and making our own plans on what we would do when the grown-ups got back. The next few weeks would be kushti for us to run wild and climb trees and gates, which we loved to dare each other to do – when we were not in the garden picking the hops. We were skilled at taking opportunities when we got the chance, so in the weeks ahead our parents would have their work cut out keeping their yocks on we four older ones, but for now we were content to be under strict orders and await their return.

While we were sat there, through the gate came a wagon followed by two trolleys loaded with many chavvies of all ages. We watched as they came to a stop just like we had, to pick out their stopping place. The father pointing this way and that, in the end they pulled in close to the gate and near the tap so it would be easier for them to get at the water – from where we were, it looked as though they had enough chavvies to drink it dry. We watched every move they made, craning our necks to get a better view of their antics. Even from the distance a-tween us, we could see that these chavvies was well used to doing their allotted jobs, with their parents hardly having to raise their voices.

'They lot is sissy cats,' said our Alfie. 'Bet yis they's sissy cats.'

For once we all agreed. These chavvies whom we did not recognise were too well behaved and not our cup of tea.

'We shan't be playing with that lot,' says Jimmy, 'they won't be no fun.'

Hark at us we was criticising a gang of chavvies for being too well behaved, which said a lot for we four baby grown-ups. Of course we would have dearly loved to wander up to their wagon and take a kushti look at them, see what things they owned. But there was a rule we dare not break or we would be in real hot water from our own parents: when a family or families pulls in anywhere it's an unwritten rule that you give them time and space to sort themselves out – once they're unpacked, then you walk over to greet and speak to them. There's always so much to do on pulling in anywhere – grys to sort out, yogs to be lit and all the unpacking of necessaries like pots and food hampers – it can be annoying to be interrupted while you're so busy sorting yourself out. We knew we would be classed as brazen if we dared walk over to these new arrivals.

There is a code of conduct within our community, and also a code of honour. In fact there are many codes we have to live by. We are always having it drummed into us: you can't do this, you can't do that. It don't always work on us, but we do know right from wrong. So we stayed put by the yog and just watched everything that was going on.

Then, once they had set up their stopping place, the father walked over to us to ask us who our family was.

'Hello, who's you lot, then?' He was smiling.

'We's the Smiths.'

'Where from?'

'Down country way,' we told him.

'What's yer dad's name?'

Some of us said 'Lenard Smith', some 'Jim Smith'.

'Oh I thinks I might know yis lot, then. We don't pick the hops here much, we picks in Kent.'

'Where's that to, then,' asked our Alfie, being the eldest of our group.

'Oh miles away, my chavvie,' answered the man.

'You got a lot of chavvies,' I had to go and say.

'Yes, me and me woman got fifteen, all alive and living. And kushti chavvies they be one and all. Well, I'll dick yis lot later,' and off he went back to tell his woman who we were.

We watched as the family put up two makeshift tents each big enough to hold a full-size wagon – one for the boys to sleep in, the other for their gals. This we knew because our boys and gals are not allowed to sleep in the same tent or wagon. They were more than a fair-sized family who would work hard for their parents, but they seemed too well-behaved to be much fun so we dismissed them as playmates. We knew many more wagons would come rolling through the gate over the next few days.

The time sped by as we kept our yocks on this new family all the while keeping our yog burning brightly and the kettles singing in the hot ashes. Then me Mam and Dad and Jim and May come driving the cart though the gate. We saw them hold up their hands in greeting to the new family but they kept on right to our part of the field.

It was kushti to have them back. 'Kettle's boiling,' we all said at once, knowing this was what they would want to hear. The weather was now turning chilly – a drop of scolding hot sloppy would be just what they needed after the cold ride back.

'Yis lot ain't been bothering they Travellers, have yis?' Jim asked, looking right at each of us in turn.

'No, we have not.'

'That's kushti then, so it means yis lot behaved yer selves.'

For being kushti we were given two bullseye sweets each. They could only get a few sweets but these were more than welcome. We'd save them to suck after we ate our fresh crusty bread and cheese, which would be our next meal.

'That Traveller man come down to dick us, Dad,' our Alfie informed him.

'That's kushti. Me an' Jim will have a chat to him later.'

That's another rule: we don't visit others while they're eating a meal. Both lots pulled on the field were now eating.

The Traveller man made the first move and walked across to our yog.

'Youse be the Smith brothers, I guess,' he said, holding out his hand.

'Kushti to meet you,' he was told as his hand were shook by our parents.

'Who's you one of?' he was asked.

'I be a Loveridge – Musher Loveridge from up country.' Past Hereford was known as 'up country'.

'Well, pleased to dick yis, Musher. I'm Lenard, this is one of me brothers, Jim,' and once again his hand was pumped up and down.

At last we four could get ourselves off to play, giving the newcomers a wide berth. We wanted no truck with they lot – they was too posh and too well-behaved for us. We could find plenty of mischief to get into without that lot.

Over the next few days both families became friends and spent many happy hours chatting and learning about each other. In fact they became lifelong friends and would meet up for the hop-picking for years after. Even though we had taken a dislike to their chavvies on sight we changed our minds once we got to know them and we four found out that their chavvies was kushti. We palled up with them to walk to the village shop, learning about each other as we walked.

Soon the field was brimming over with wagons and tents as old friends and members of our family pulled in from all over the country. Among them me Dad's brothers, John, Joe, Alfie, Dan and Jessie. Tom, me Dad's other brother, had stayed behind to keep Granny and Grandad company while the others came to work in the gardens. Because Tom had stayed back, his brothers would put by a couple of shillings a week to give to him on their return so that he too would get a share of the hop-picking. It was taken for granted that if one brother in a family stayed behind to keep an eye on the old folks, he would not lose by it.

Andrew and Dinea Bowers, some of the Coopers and Loveridges, some Hughes and many more from Somerset and Wiltshire, Dorset, Devon and Cornwall had travelled up to the hop gardens. It was like one big extended family because everybody knew each other. There were also other families from faraway-sounding areas with names that meant little to us at that time. Years later that would all change, when we Romanies became motorised. Then we would travel to places in one day that it used to take us months to reach – and we would meet up with people from so much farther afield.

All that was in the future, though. For now, on a cold, damp, misty morning we walked the short distance to the hop garden and chose the crib we would pick our hops in. We would stick to this same crib for the season as did all the rest of the pickers. Me Mam had kept warm clothes and wellington boots packed away for months (that she had begged over the summer), ready for us to wear for the hops. Most of the mothers did the same – our welfare was thought of well in advance. Mothers always put their chavvies before themselves as a matter of course and our Mam was well prepared for this hard season. She even had some suitable clothes for me Dad to work in.

We had already walked the hop gardens while out playing with other chavvies, so this early morning was not our first sight of the damp hops hanging in big bunches on the vines. Me Dad had to lift me up onto the side of the crib; our Alfie was tall enough to climb on by himself. Jim was doing likewise with his little brood, sitting them on the side of the crib. Our dads would pull down the vines for us to pick clean of the hops, which we would then drop into the crib. Twice a day the farmer would bushel off the hops in me Dad's name – he had a round basket that held one bushel and we needed to pick as many bushels as possible each day, just as we needed to pick a good number of nets of peas in the pea-picking season. It all boiled down to: keep at it. Every hop counted – pennies and shillings must be earned. This was the last chance of the year to line the pockets of those who had no winter work – and there were many who didn't.

We had not been at it long before that little mush our Alfie got the bright idea of lighting a yog so we could have our breakfast.

'Hush and carry on. It's still too early yet,' he was told.

Good try, our Alfie, I wish it had worked for I too was beginning to get cold and shivery sitting on the crib. In fact I was worse than useless early on a morning, but I was being petted by me Dad to keep picking off the smelly hops.

'But Dad, I only got dear little hands and they's as cold as a frog.'

'Keep picking. Come Christmas, I'll buy yis a big dolly.'

Time meaning nothing to me, I told him Christmas was years away and I didn't want no dolly anyway. I wanted to go back to the wagon. After a few hugs, kisses, dire threats and big promises from me Dad, I settled down to slowly pick me hops. Me Mam kept out of our ups and downs, leaving it to me Dad to sort me out the best he could. Even as chavvies we knew the importance of working and how it enabled us to live, to shoe our grys, repair our wagons and paint them once a year. So we was taught to earn vonger by hawking or doing groundwork from an early age. So picking these hops was part of everyday life and we accepted it as such.

It was not only the Gypsy community working in the gardens. There were families with children the same age as us picking the hops who were house-dwellers. They came down from big towns to earn money. If you're really desperate for vonger, the season seems very short – too short to earn the amount the gorgies need. Not all the gorgies was so desperate – a few came on a working holiday, as they called it, but they all lived in the farm buildings, away from our field. Some of them said quite openly that they wished they too had their homes with them.

Theirs was a harder season than ours, for we had our comforts with us and our day-to-day life changed little. We was glad of the work, too. Some Travellers who were late getting there was turned away – the farmer had his number of pickers, so they was forced to seek out less popular farms to work on.

For such a small group, compared to families with ten or fifteen chavvies, me Dad thought we were doing very well. Big families were the thing back then: lots of families had ten chavvies or more, all ready to pitch in and work. Big vonger could be earned by big families. This work in the hop gardens was taken very seriously.

Each day the baker, butcher and milkman called on the field, and once a week the fish man would come, so there was little need to run to the shops. The farmer would sell us eggs and butter, sometimes cheese.

To me the best part of the day was stopping for breakfast, sitting on the hop vines which had been picked clean of hops, round a brilliant hot yog, getting warmed up inside and out.

Eggs and bacon with fried taters was the meal for us. Some families fried kippers bought off the fish man, but we only had kippers when me Mam had time to pick all the little bones out in case we got choked to death. And there was no time for that while out on the garden. There was just no time to waste – it was eat, drink, then back to the hop crib.

We were just a couple of weeks into the season when we had a pair of runaways – a young boy and gal who could not wait to get their parents onside to get married. They went to the pictures on a Friday night and never returned. Both sets of parents went berserk and I'm sure would have moured the pair of them if only they could have got their hands on them. The field was in uproar when the mothers discovered them missing, fathers jumping on grys to ride off bareback looking for them. But they had planned it well and could not be found. The other men on the field tormented the families of the two kids by telling them to work extra hard as they would have a wedding to pay for in the near future. This didn't go down too well because of the shame that was brought down on the parents by what their offspring had done – even though many that were doing the tormenting had themselves been runaways years back. I know me Mam and Dad ran away during the pea-picking season. And some young couples choose the hop-picking season to do it.

But when runaways were found, their parents usually made them get married. It still happens today. My nephew ran away with his gal friend four years ago; they too was brought back and made to marry. Marriage is taken very seriously in our community. Most married couples are only parted by death: marriage is a contract we make for life and we keep to it. We did not see the young couple again – they were keeping their heads down, knowing they had caused a scandal in their families, but we did hear there was a wedding in the new year, so all ended well for them.

The weeks flew by and a great many bushels of hops got picked. Down in our little corner of the field we had made it homely: we had old petrol cans to sit on of an evening round the yog and there'd be visits to other yogs to join in the singing and dancing that occurred most nights. On Saturday nights we chavvies sat outside the village kitcherma while the grown-ups let their hair down. While we were sitting on the wall we gals would spy young couples getting to know each other. If any of the parents caught them being too friendly sparks would fly. Of course these boys and gals were much older than me and Lilea and our group but we still noticed things like a sly kiss or holding hands. And to see a boy put his arms round the gal – oh my, this was really bad and not allowed, for if found out both would be in for a hiding and make no mistake about that – but we knew how to keep our mouths shut. We never told on anyone. That way we would not be known as tell-tits, for once you got a reputation as a tell-tit you would lose your friends. Trust means a great deal in our community.

You would think that, once they came out the kitcherma, after singing and dancing all evening, they would want to fall into bed. Not they – it all started again once they were back on the field, singing and dancing for half the night, with many a sore head come morning. Did they learn from this? No, they was soon awaiting the next Saturday night to come round, when they did it all over again. I think having dozens of different families for company had a lot to do with it.

Some of the funny things that were said come to mind: 'Get out the road, let me woman show you how to step dance,' or, 'Hark up, let me woman sing, she's just like a nightingale' only to hear what sounded like a frog croaking once they did all hark. But some of our lot had grand voices and could really sing a kushti old-fashioned song or two. As for step dancing, most men, women and chavvies could make music on the boards with their feet. It's something that comes natural to us from an early age and then right through our lives.

Left to our own devices, we're a happy band of people who entertain each other at all times, be it telling old tales, dancing or singing. That's our kind of entertainment and brings happiness to one and all. Another form of entertainment for us was watching the men deal among themselves or chopping out one gry for another. As there was Travellers from far and wide who had not seen particular grys pulling wagons, the men would stand and swear on their lives how kushti this gry or that gry was, in the hope of selling it. You should have heard the oaths that were sworn: 'On me dead father, that gry is one hundred percent,' and his father would be stood in the crowd, not dead at all. Or, 'Strike me stone dead if I'm not telling the truth, my brother.' Yes, it could be fun to stand and watch the men dealing with each other. This mostly happened on a Sunday morning while the women were boiling their washing snow white, just to show up any woman whose washing was considered below standard.

Me Mam was one of the main culprits. She would boil her teatowels and nappies (though not in the same bucket) for hours, just to show up everyone else. There was a certain pride in everything me Mam did and her wagon was a sight to behold, so clean and neat (as were most wagons). And there was another reason too: because of the bitterness of me Dad's old Mum and his sister towards me Mam, she always made sure she was on top of her cleaning and washing. As for us chavvies, our mams made our lives a misery with washing us day and night. Give them their due, our mothers kept their offspring in tiptop condition in every way, and although we chavvies grumbled at being washed so much, it stood us in good stead for when we grew up, because we did the same to our own chavvies and homes. Our mams bred pride in us. But, believe me, being washed round the yog in the winter months was no joke, but it always livened us up and at least we were clean. In frost and snow she would take the tin bath up into the wagon so we got washed in front of the queenie stove. The wagon being as warm as toast, we sure did get a good scrubbing.

The weather was turning colder now, as the hop season progressed but, being Romani, we were used to getting on with whatever the weather or life threw our way. When you're in the last few days of a job such as hop-picking and know that you will not see some of the Travellers who live in other parts of the country again for a long while (especially if there are very old individuals) you can start to feel sad. There may be deaths we won't hear about until the next season – and all these families have become kushti friends over many years hop-picking together. Me Mam was particularly fond of some older folk who lived on the opposite side of the country from us. In they days that seemed like thousands of miles away, another world.

Anything could happen from one season to the next. Many groups feared their young men and women would meet and marry up with someone whose family came from far away – they could lose contact so easily, just like me Grandad's sister Bertha, who met and married someone and went off to rear her own family, but was not seen again by her own family. This happened some time in the late Thirties or early Forties. The family she married into was from the Evesham area and it was only in the last decade that contact was made with her children, when I helped her granddaughter, Sallyann Smith, with some planning. It was her father who made the connection between us. How pleased dear old Grandad, who died in the Fifties, would have been to hear that his lost sister had had a good life and a wonderful family. I know that there had always been great worry over me Dad's Aunt Bertha, not knowing whether she was dead or alive. Yet, when we went hop-picking we must have travelled through her adopted area without knowing it. For weeks on end we could have met up with her and her new family but never did.

Sallyann's Dad has brought us up to date now though. Bertha met and married a Romani by the name of Bill Smith. Bill and Bertha had five sons, one of whom, Dolphie, is Sallyann's Dad and better known as Frogger. Then there was George and Shaddie, Freddie and Fisher. Fisher lost his life in his thirties during the hop-picking season when the cart he was in turned over. So Bertha knew sorrow as well as happiness. But her mother and father, brothers and sisters knew nothing of all this.

I keep in touch with my Uncle Frogger and Aunt Tanner through Sallyann and her husband Dennie. I have been to their site up in Evesham and had a great surprise, for Frogger's family are old-fashioned and wagon-builders to boot, which would have pleased me Dad no end. If only he had been alive to meet his cousin Frogger and family – all them wasted years when we could have got to know our extended family and they us. I think me Dad would have had his dealing head on if he had met Frogger, for when the family showed me their coloured grys – kushti little tits – me Dad's mouth would have watered for a deal or chop out.

Over the generations these permanent partings happened in so many of our close-knit family groups.

The field was beginning to thin out as families set off on the tober back to their parts of the country. I watched as with tears in their yocks each family made their farewells and the wagons slowly set off through the gate.

'Oh well,' said me Dad to Jim, 'that's it fer another year, then. Kushti friends must part.'

'You's right there, our Lenard, some of they lot is the salt of the earth. It's been kushti knowing 'em.'

Our lot waited a couple of days before pulling out, giving the others time to get ahead on their way back to wherever they come from.

'What's we gonna do, then, our Jim?' asked me Dad.

'Well, I reckons we should give our Jessie, Joe and Dan and John time to get well on the tober afore we starts back, because too many going the same way will bring us nothing but trouble from the gavvers. Yeah, and there's all the Devon lot and the rest of the down-country lot travelling back as well.'

And so we waited for the tobers to clear a bit. When our two wagons pulled out and made our way back to the main road, me Dad's yocks lingered on the village kitcherma as we passed it by. The landlord's takings would fall to the floor now the Gypsies had left. 'Oh well,' he would sigh, 'there's always next year.'

On our long journey back, me and Lilea went out hawking the wooden flowers with our mams while the wagons pulled in and waited for us. Then off we would go again, each day another village to call. We had good calling on the way back down to Wiltshire, as most families' pockets was well greased with their earnings and they did not bother to knock on doors. But pockets can soon get thin when the long winter is on us, as our lot would say, and so we hawked our way back down to Devizes and pulled in on one of the wide verges while the two men went off seeking farm work.

'I hope they gets lucky, my May. The wind here is enough to cut yer throat. We could do with a bit of shelter.'

'Well, let's cross our fingers, my Vie, and hope for the best.'

They found work cutting wood into logs and the farmer let us pull close to the farmyard and use an open-sided barn to put up a washing line – as the wind whistled through it dried the clothes and there was shelter from the rain too. So we fared very well, as luck would have it.

Christmas come but I did not get the big dolly me Dad had promised me. I was quick to remind him but he said I would get one when we went to the first fair of the year – he would win me one if I was a kushti gal. I knew he meant well but, once at the fair, we would be lucky to dick him till nightfall.

'I'll never get me no dolly, Dad, and you knows it.'

'Don't cry, my gal, you'll get one, I promise.'

But I never did get that dolly or the dear little dolls' house I craved. Well I did, but I was sixty years old by then.

Chapter Eighteen

Springtime Comes Around Again

THE WINTER WENT WELL. We had a fall of snow but not as bad as some years past and the men was still earning a few shillings each week. Our grys, fed on meadow hay, did well too.

Then came the day in February when we were ready move on to seek out the first of the wild snowdrops. The farmer had done us proud and wanted us to stay on working, but needs must and our minds was already deep in the snowdrop copse. Tradition holds firm with us lot and it's traditional that our year really starts with the first wild flowers, free for one and all to pick. So we made our cold way to the Wiltshire copse that we knew so well, pulled in and lit the yog.

Spying another wagon up the narrow lane, it dawned on us who it was – me Dad's brother John, who soon come to our yog as he had recognised us the instant we pulled in. This would be fun as his older gals would come picking with us.

There was a watery bit of sun shining on the lane, but once deep in the copse there was white frost still on the ground and stuck fast to the tree trunks and branches. The little wild snowdrops grew in abundance throughout the copse – great patches glowed under the brambles.

'Mam?'

'What, my Maggie?'

'Why is it these flowers picks the thorny brambles to grow under, eh?'

'I don't know, my gal, but pick 'em all the same. It's as bad fer us lot as it is fer you, so get yer back to it and start picking.'

Jimmy, Robert and our Alfie rambled away as they picked, which meant that, for once, I would not be pushed arse over tip in the brambles when me and that little mush our Alfie got at it. We would fall out and come to blows at least once a day, no matter what work or game we was at. But, even though we would nearly mour each other when we fell out, each was the first to stick up for the other against anyone else who fancied a rough and tumble.

How I loved these little wild flowers and felt it a shame to pull them from their copse where they grew so happily to end up on a table or windowsill where it was too hot for them to breathe. They were wild things that wanted to stay out in the wild but, as me Mam told me, the house-dwellers liked to buy them to brighten their homes and it earned us a living. Once bunched and backed with sprays of box, these flowers looked grand and we could sell as many as we could pick.

The great clumps of flowers in the copse were a wonderful sight, untouched till we lot arrived to pick them. Nature is a marvellous thing to behold in each new season – it gladdens the yocks and heart. And when the yocks of the house-dwellers fell on our hawking baskets full of blooms for the first time, it gladdened their yocks and hearts too. They opened their doors and looked at the flowers before looking to see who was selling them. Mind you, we holds the baskets in front of us so they can't miss them, really. Nine times out of ten, the sight of the flowers will bring us a sale: they can't resist them.

The boys in our family groups rarely came out selling the flowers; it was us elder gals and our mams. We had to dress up warm, for you quickly got chilled tramping from door to door. Sometimes we would be offered a hot drink – but not often enough – and sometimes one of our women would beg or buy a pot of hot tea, but we would carefully pick a nice clean house to ask for it. Then we huddled up and drank the tea and ate any biscuits or cake offered. Although the cold affected us, it was worse for the gorgies for we lot was weathered and felt it less than they did. So it was a chilly group that called the outlying villages and made some of the dwelling-house lot happy and some very angry because we had the nerve to knock on their doors. Oh well, you can't please everyone – at least we don't seem to be able to.

Then it was time to move on to the wild daffies. Again, a much-admired little wild flower. These were easier to pick and more accessible – the part of the big wood where the flowers grew was not so dark or dense as the snowdrop copse: the woodmen and gamekeeper did well to keep it clear. But in other parts of the wood one could easily get lost. It was such a big old place, part of an old estate with a huge house in it where rich folks lived. And there was us Travellers picking their flowers to sell – if only they had known. But the gamekeeper knew: he would let certain families pick the flowers and others he would threaten to shoot stone dead, so our little group was lucky to be known to him and be given a couple of days to help ourselves to the flowers. But he made sure we moved on and left his area when the time was up. Like me Dad said, if we caused no trouble, then we got none in return. So we would shift on our way once more, with our little wild daffodils bunched up and ready to hawk round the doors, and everyone was happy.

After picking basket after basket of primroses and cowslips, when they too came in season, and enjoying a bit of warmer weather, we continued to travel – down through Frome, Shepton Mallet and Glastonbury and on to Bridgwater ready to pick the peas. Most of the lanes and grass verges had wagons full of happy families pulled on them, all getting ready to travel to the farm of their choice to pick the season. Bridgwater town would once again be full of travelling Gypsies passing through, heading for their chosen work-place. It would once again be overrun each Saturday with families shopping and drinking – the townspeople never minded because our lot would have kushti vonger to spend.

The pea fields meant a great deal to me, because I had been born on one. Yes, right in the middle of the season, one fine July day, surrounded by many families and acres of green peas. So I felt really at home on the pea fields each year as I grew up. And when I grew older and picked on the very field, I was told, 'That spot over there, Maggie, is where you come into the world.' So I knew the very spot the wagon had stood on when I got meself born. In these days very few babies was born in a hospital – most of us was born in wagons or tents out in the countryside.

Once we was allowed to pull on the pea field and settle in, we would have our first fresh picked peas of the season with our meal. There was a little saying said by many:

Thank the Lord for what I've had
If it was more, I would be glad

Which made me smile each time I heard it, but it was our way of thanking the good Lord for providing food. These little sayings was always repeated for each new season's food, be it swede, peas or cabbage.

Although I enjoyed going out hawking with me Mam, I think pea-picking was one of me favourite times of year. During the day, all we chavvies would have our own rolled-down nets to pick in and would be coaxed or threatened to keep picking the peas off the plants and fill the net. As we grew older it would turn into a competition as to which of us could pick the most nets each day. This pleased our parents no end: the more we picked the more they earned.

After the day's work, we'd be shelling peas or broad beans or peeling the taters for our mams, then running off to play with dozens of other chavvies while the food was cooked and the washing done and hung on the hedge to dry. Then we'd be made to cry when it was our turn to be washed and our hair combed out and re-plaited, ready for the next day.

If the weather was kind and we had a lot of sunshine, the evenings would be that much longer for get-togethers round the old yog. I always found the old tales that were being repeated for the hundredth time interesting and entertaining. Sad tales that would make me yocks leak, funny tales that would have us rolling in laughter, ghost tales that would give us a shiver up the spine and make the hair on our necks stand up. Men and women with their chavvies would stroll over to other families' yogs and settle down for a few hours of well-earned entertainment. It cost nothing to be happy and enjoy each other's company. Enjoy ourselves we did.

There was often a wedding and a few punch-ups to settle old feuds as well during the season.

This then was the life of the Romani Gypsies when we travelled the highways of our areas. We were more than independent and lived according to our own lifestyle. Wherever possible we kept ourselves to ourselves. We Gypsies now are still struggling to do the same whilst living in today's society. But we must never forget the original group that landed on these shores back in the fourteenth century who made it possible for us to continue our race. I hope this account of our history and unique hard way of life will give the settled communities a better window through which to view the old Romani Gypsy race, to have a little more understanding of our traditional way of life, our culture, customs and traditions.

For what our forefathers suffered, it's time now for us to be accepted, to live side by side in peace with our gorgie neighbours … after all these years.

Acknowledgements

ONE LADY STANDS OUT: Rachel Francis-Ingham. Rachel runs the UK Association of Gypsy Women up in Darlington. The work this lady and her team does is second to none. I have known her on many occasions to sit up right through the night working on a case, then get into her office next morning to start on another. Rachel will take on health, access problems, education and homeless Gypsies looking for a pitch as well as supporting Gypsies in other countries such as Kosovo where she and her group funds food and clothing and even firewood for the really poor Gypsies. This is the pure dedication of a Romani Gypsy for her race. My nickname for her is 'My old gal' – we are best of friends as well as working colleagues. God bless you, Rachel, for helping so many of our people in need of guidance and help.

Chris Johnson and the barrister Marc Willers of the Birmingham Law Group are the people up front who takes the brunt of changes in government policy. These two work like gophers, always challenging new policies and working to win planning applications countrywide.

They help hundreds of families each year one way or another, which to me is remarkable for these two well-known men are gorgies who have chosen to help my race and many others. I take me hat off to the pair of you.

To Dr Angus Murdoch, who is a great and much appreciated planning consultant here in the West Country and a kushti friend who has taken heavy workloads off my shoulders, thank you, Angus, for being you.

To my friend, New Traveller Simon Rushton, MA MA MRTPI, my grateful thanks to you who saves me life, sorting out my computer.

To a very special man and friend, my Lord Avebury, who has worked so hard for the Gypsy and Traveller communities for too many years to count. He is indeed a very special man and a lovely person.

And a big heartfelt thank you to every one of those people that supported me to be included in the Queen's Birthday Honours list to receive the BEM medal. It's a great honour to receive this medal and it will, I hope, give my community a big boost to look to the future.

Kushti bok (Good luck) to one and all.

Glossary of Romani Words

allum pea-plant

bok luck

chavvy child

to chop to swap or barter

to dick to see

dinalow fool

doughty dear, as in 'oh dear'

effet lizard

gavver policeman

to gin to know

gorgie non-Romani

gry horse

gub witch

juckle dog

kitcherma pub

kushti good

to mour to kill

to muller to die

mush man

nixis nothing

shussy rabbit

staadi hat

stralk potato

sutty sleep

tan place or house

vellie centre of a wheel

vonger money

yock eye

yog fire

youry egg

Reading List: Romani History

The Gypsies by Angus Fraser (Blackwell, 1995). A well-respected broad history.

Gypsies under the Swastika by Donald Kenrick and Grattan Puxon (University of Hertfordshire Press, 2009). An overview of the Nazi persecution of the Gypsies.

Shared Sorrows: A Gypsy family remembers the Holocaust by Toby Sonneman (University of Hertfordshire Press, 2002). The story of a Gypsy family interweaved with that of a Jewish family in Nazi Germany.

Stopping Places: A Gypsy history of South London and Kent by Simon Evans (University of Hertfordshire Press, 2004). Includes vivid first-hand accounts of the traditional life of Gypsies on their rounds of seasonal agricultural work. With 170 photos.

The Traveller-Gypsies by Judith Okely (Cambridge University Press, 1998). A sympathetic study of Gypsies past and present by a respected social anthropologist.

We are the Romani people: Ames am e Rromane dzene by Ian Hancock (University of Hertfordshire Press, 2002). A passionate and very readable account of Gypsy history and culture by a leading Gypsy academic and campaigner against anti-Gypsy prejudice.

Winter Time: Memoirs of a German Sinto who survived Auschwitz by Walter Winter (University of Hertfordshire Press, 2004). A very moving autobiography.